Contents

Introduction

To the Mormon reader,

My initial objective in composing this work is to educate the Mormon reader. Sadly, many church-members have a limited grasp of the doctrines they profess to believe and often even shy away from the "hard" questions, choosing to "have faith" instead of seeking understanding (are they scared of what they will find?). Often I hear individuals in the church express understandably misguided, yet typically well-intentioned ideas similar to '…it doesn't matter [the answer to a "hard" question], as long as you have faith. The Lord knows and that is sufficient.'

However, the LORD himself has said, "Yea behold, I will tell you in your *mind* and in your heart" and "…*seek learning*, even by *study* and also by *faith*" (D&C 8:2, D&C 88:118, emphasis added). He expects us to seek understanding, even when it 'doesn't make a difference to our eternal salvation.'

Of course, we cannot expect to understand everything and at times faith is all we *can* have. Nevertheless, we can, and should, always seek for additional insight (Cook, 2008). For example, I have "faith" that the tides will come in and out every day following a recurring pattern. However, knowing how they are affected by the gravity of the moon (and the sun to a much lesser extent) enhances my understanding and even increases my "faith" that the tides will not suddenly stop tomorrow or change their pattern (Tides and Water Levels, 2017).

This is especially true when I encounter a phenomenon that seems to contradict my belief. If I accept as true that the tides occur based only on what I have been told or what "feels" right, what then if I discover a circumstance in which the tides should, but do not seem to exist, such as in a river or lake? I might choose to naively exercise my "faith" and ignore this seemingly contradictory occurrence, justifying my lack of further study with the notion that 'the Lord knows the answer.' Or I can educate myself further regarding this mystery, recognizing that I already "believe" in tides and so it would seem prudent to determine how my "belief" relates to this peculiar situation.

This investigation would inevitably lead me to the knowledge that there indeed exists a tide of sorts in all lakes and rivers as they are affected by the gravitational pull of the moon, as are the oceans. However, in a lake or river, the effect of gravity on such a relatively small body of water is so trivial as to be very nearly undetectable (Do the Great Lakes Have Tides?, 2017).

Likewise, we may already know the gospel is true, so when we encounter something that seems to contradict our belief, just "having faith" that the Lord knows the answer is a lazy-man's approach. The Lord often desires, or at least allows us to know as well, but ordinarily we are obliged to seek for clarification ourselves, although the solution may not be found in a church building so-to-speak (Kimball, 1983). Instead, curiosity and effort are oftentimes the key ingredients in deciphering the way in which the answer to a question coincides with the truths you already embrace.

In other words, although you may have faith in something that is actually true, is that faith not limited by your willingness to ignore that which is beyond your current, but attainable knowledge? Rather than making excuses for gospel tenets such as polygamy and our potential as gods, better is to understand them and be able to defend them (Keetch, 2017)! Please understand that I am not advocating Biblical warfare, but I am suggesting that a more complete awareness of the doctrines of our faith, even those in which we prefer to avoid discussing with our various non-member associates, ought to an objective of significant importance.

In any event, this book was written for the purpose of helping you to gain a greater understanding of those thing that you already have faith in, from the perspective of those that currently accept the Bible as the *only* word of God. After all, if the doctrines we claim are those of God Almighty, but fail to appear in the Bible, then we truly do have little more than blind faith, we are simply fortunate enough to blindly be following that which is indeed true.

To the non-Mormon reader,

The second purpose of this book is to enhance the understanding of honest, truth-seeking people not of the Mormon faith. Although this work is written as if to the Mormon reader alone, it can still provide significant insights into our faith with that context in mind. There are many that disagree with our doctrines, and that may include you, but it is only fair that you understand our justification for them, not just the sometimes non-sensical and false perceptions that often exist.

The 'tried-and-true' answer that I am supposed to provide to you is to read the Book of Mormon and pray to God with full intent regarding its truthfulness. When God answers in the affirmative, then by implication, you will also know that its translator, Joseph Smith, must have truly been a prophet to produce such a work, that the church he restored is currently led by Christ himself through a modern-day prophet and lastly, that the tenets of the church are divinely inspired as well.

I personally maintain these beliefs, but as a rationally driven individual I also recognize that although a witness from God is paramount to one's comprehension of truth, the above-mentioned scenario is probably not what has driven you to read this work, and that is acceptable to me. My intention is not to convert you, but rather to inform you; better me than someone not even of the Mormon faith. As such I have chosen to exclusively quote from the Bible as a source of doctrine and scripture, as I suppose you already believe it is true, as do we.

In short, you may find our faith to be obscure, non-doctrinal and even unchristian, but we do not consider that our unique beliefs were some invention of Joseph Smith. We believe that Joseph Smith *restored* the Church of Christ, not founded a new one, in which case none of the "new" doctrines he introduced would be new at all. They should be consistent with those found in the original church established some 2000 years ago by Jesus Christ himself, about which the Holy Bible provides a direct account.

Please allow me to clarify further: If our church is indeed the restored Church of Christ, then there ought to exist evidence of our unique doctrines within the pages of the Bible. Although you may not entirely agree with the interpretation of the scriptures that I present, I invite you to at least attempt to understand our perspective in an intellectually honest way.

Ch. 1: The Great Apostasy

Mormons believe in what is referred to as the Great Apostasy, in which the original Church of Christ was eventually lost after the Apostles died and a multitude of differing ideas about God and his gospel became commonplace (Oaks D. H., 1995).

The Catholic Church asserts that Paul passed the torch onto the ancient fathers up to today, with an unbroken line of authority (Peter and the Papacy, 2017), but a review of the history of the Catholic Church over the centuries casts doubt on this claim considering the volume of bloodshed and carnage (especially among themselves) spurred by the Church claiming to represent Christ (Eberhart, 2009).

Assuming any Pope of antiquity truly wielded the authority of God, could we not assume that his license to speak in God's name became void when he committed the most atrocious acts of violence and immorality? After all, many of the Popes who supposedly succeeded Peter are well-known for their realization of great acts of this sordid nature (Tharoor, Ishaan, 2015) Please do not misunderstand my intentions, I do not wish to suggest that the Catholic Church of today nor its people are immoral or otherwise evil; to the contrary. I only wish to propose that the behavior of their early leadership invalidates any claims to an unbroken line of authority originating with the Apostle Peter, had one existed in the first place.

This 'falling away,' as it is commonly referred to in the Mormon faith, is our explanation for why so many conflicting Christian faiths, all claiming to teach the true gospel of Jesus Christ, exist today. Over the centuries, organizers honestly attempting to spread what they deem to be the word of God, and others perhaps seeking power and wealth, have established churches to convey their interpretation of God's teachings to their followers, naturally leading to the presence of thousands of organizations, each differing from one another, even if only in minor ways (About the World Christian Database, 2017). Now if no falling away had occurred, then Mormonism would be rightfully deemed a counterfeit since we hold that the Church of Jesus Christ of Latter-day Saints is the *restored* gospel; the *same* organization that Christ himself established (Underwood, 2002).

Perhaps the most ironic element in our discussion of the Great Apostasy is that all Christians, save Catholics, fail to realize that just such an event is critical to their faith. If indeed the Catholic church is the same organization Christ established, then it is His and all the others must be, at best, erroneous variations and at worst, imposters. This being the case, all other Christian faiths must have arrived later, or as break-off. But, if Catholicism is a warped version of the original church, then the truth must have been lost. There can really be no other option.

Following this same line of reasoning, that if there is indeed a church that is entirely consistent to the one Christ established 2,000 years ago, it must be either the Catholic church (assuming an unbroken line of authority from Peter to the current Pope) or the Mormons (assuming the line was broken and then restored through Joseph Smith.)

Now that we have constructed a rational basis for this so-called apostasy, it is equally important to note that Bible itself speaks of just such events occurring, including the Great Apostasy upon which the validity of the Mormon faith rests so heavily.

Amos :11-12

11 ¶ Behold, the days come, saith the Lord GOD, that I will send a famine in the land, not a famine of bread, nor a thirst for water, but of hearing the words of the LORD:

12 And they shall wander from sea to sea, and from the north even to the east, they shall run to and fro to seek the word of the LORD, and shall not find it.

Within these verses, Amos declares that there will come a time in which people will seek God's Word but will not find it. Obviously, if they *cannot* find it, then it must not be find-able. Now when could this happen? It must have transpired following Amos, who prophesied around 750BC although we cannot be certain it speaks of the Great Apostasy without greater detail (New World Encyclopedia, 2017). Allow me to explain: We often assume that the Word of God, however you may define that term, has always existed, but that is not necessarily true. Mormon scholars suggest that there have been many times in which the truth of God was absent from the earth, or at least an entire people, typically because of its rejection (Compton, 2007).

For example, The New Testament illustrates just how spiritually corrupted the Jews had become when Jesus entered the scene, so perhaps the truth had already been lost by the time of His ministry and this is the apostasy that Amos is articulating. At the very least, Amos is suggesting that there will be a time when the word of God does not exist on earth, something that has probably happened more than once throughout history. So, while whether or not this prophecy refers to the Great Apostasy is debatable, it does suggest that at the very least there is a precedence for such an event.

Matthew 16:27

40 When the lord therefore of the vineyard cometh, what will he do unto those husbandmen?

41 They say unto him, He will miserably destroy those wicked men, and will let out his vineyard unto other husbandmen, which shall render him the fruits in their seasons.

42 Jesus saith unto them, Did ye never read in the scriptures, The stone which the builders rejected, the same is become the head of the corner: this is the Lord's doing, and it is marvellous in our eyes?

43 Therefore say I unto you, The kingdom of God shall be taken from you, and given to a nation bringing forth the fruits thereof.

These verses constitute the end of the parable of the husbandmen, who wreaked havoc in the vineyard in the absence of their master. Upon his return, he destroys these wicked servants and leases out the vineyard to others who can be trusted. These others are those who accept him as their chief and will deliver him "fruits," or righteous works.

As with all of His parables, Jesus intends a deeper meaning that extends far beyond the day-to-day of vineyard employees. In verse 43 the vineyard is identified as a representation of the Kingdom of God and that it will be given to another nation. Christ is speaking to the Jews, so there is little doubt that His suggestion is that the Kingdom of God will be taken from them and given to another nation. Granted, it does not identify this nation, although it would be reasonable to assume the future United States, there is no doubt that it will be taken from the Jews. When did this happen according to the standard Christian historical timeline?

Matthew 24:23-24

23 Then if any man shall say unto you, Lo, here is Christ, or there; believe it not.

24 For there shall arise false Christs, and false prophets, and shall shew great signs and wonders; insomuch that, if it were possible, they shall deceive the very elect.

No doubt Jesus does not specifically identify a future apostasy here, but the implication of such is quite strong. What He does say is that there will be many falsehoods circulating, indicating that at least some folks have been deceived. If there was a general falling away, a Great Apostasy, then there is little doubt that this would be precisely the case; lies and fabrications galore. This is very descriptive of our day, in which there are thousands of *differing* belief systems that each claim to have the Gospel of Jesus Christ (Randall, 2017).

Acts 20:29-30

29 For I know this, that after my departing shall grievous wolves enter in among you, not sparing the flock.

30 Also of your own selves shall men arise, speaking perverse things, to draw away disciples after them.

To be fair, Paul does not specifically state here that an apostasy was looming. But what he does reveal is that *after* he leaves, "wolves" will enter the flock. It is implied by the use of a dangerous creature such as a wolf, as opposed to a fuzzy bunny or cute puppy, that the people represented by this term are not intent on building the kingdom. Understand that Paul was required to travel great distances utilizing primitive modes of transportation and thus was unable to personally attend to the various churches on any sort of regular basis. It is therefore likely that much could change by his next visit and he is warning that this would in fact be the case, but not in the fuzzy bunny sort-of way.

2 Thessalonians 2:1-3

1 Now we beseech you, brethren, by the coming of our Lord Jesus Christ, and by our gathering together unto him,

2 That ye be not soon shaken in mind, or be troubled, neither by spirit, nor by word, nor by letter as from us, as that the day of Christ is at hand.

11

3 Let no man deceive you by any means: for that day shall not come, except there come a falling away first, and that man of sin be revealed, the son of perdition;

This is one of the most powerful scriptures supporting the premise of a Great Apostasy. In this address to the Thessalonians, Paul is clearly speaking of the return, or second coming, of Christ. His followers were aware that He would return in the future, but it seems that often how far in the future was rather unclear. Although Paul does not give any sort of timeline, or even ball-park style estimate, he does make it clear that this event will *only* occur *after* a 'falling away' happens first. We can all probably agree, save the Jehovah's Witness faith, that Christ is still yet to return to rule and so this 'falling away' must have occurred in the nearly 2000 years since this scripture was written (1914—A Significant Year in Bible Prophecy, 2018).

1 Timothy 4:1-4

1 Now the Spirit speaketh expressly, that in the latter times some shall depart from the faith, giving heed to seducing spirits, and doctrines of devils;

2 Speaking lies in hypocrisy; having their conscience seared with a hot iron;

3 Forbidding to marry, and commanding to abstain from meats, which God hath created to be received with thanksgiving of them which believe and know the truth.

The book of Timothy is another set of letters written by Paul, this time not surprisingly to his friend and traveling companion, Timothy (Newton, 2017). He speaks of a time when some ill-intentioned parties, described as hypocrites and liars will be seduced by Satan and spread various "doctrines of devils". He states that two of these deceitful creeds are that marriage and eating meat are both to be avoided . Sound like our day at all?

Timothy further affirms these lies will be dispersed in the "latter times," in other words, in the future. Now to be fair, we can only be certain that this refers to sometime following Paul's proclamation, but there has only really been one time in history when the idea of marriage has been challenged altogether; now!

2 Timothy 4:3-4

3 For the time will come when they will not endure sound doctrine; but after their own lusts shall they heap to themselves teachers, having itching ears;

4 And they shall turn away their ears from the truth, and shall be turned unto fables.

Here Paul repeats himself to Timothy regarding an apostasy, mirroring the last scripture. Clearly it is a time that "will come," so it is the future in relation to Paul in which people will be turned from the truth. In fact, he specifically states that they will reject true doctrines, choosing instead to place their confidence in falsehoods. Once the apostles were killed and the leadership of the church was gone, truth was no longer defined by God, but by man. Although some of these "men" were likely well-intentioned in their mistaken understanding of God's Word, no doubt some were happy to offer a new interpretation in order to gain money or power or satisfy personal preferences.

Revelation 13:7

7 And it was given unto him to make war with the saints, and to overcome them: and power was given him over all kindreds, and tongues, and nations.

Revelation is not known to be the easiest book to understand and I will not pretend to be an expert but let us identify what it undeniably reveals. John is writing about Satan, just before he writes about Christ's second coming. He states that the devil will "overcome" the Saints, in other words, defeat them. Now this would have to happen after John, but prior to today, so when is it? I think we can all agree, Mormon or not, that we are living in the 'last days.' Consequently this event John is referring to would need to happen between his time and ours and we would be hard pressed to argue that another time than suggested by a Great Apostasy after the time of Christ makes much sense.

Ch. 2: Biblical Shortcomings

I'm not going to make many non-Mormon friends with this one, because quite frankly I will suggest that the Bible is NOT the flawless word of God. Now that you are shocked and perhaps offended, please hear me out. First let me explain what I am NOT saying. I am NOT saying the Bible is uninspired, unscriptural or unreliable, but to understand the Bible from an honest and objective standpoint, one must understand where it came from. Here's a very brief synopsis and just for the record, Mormons do believe the Bible to be the word of God, just not the ONLY word of God (Smith, 2013):

Inspired men, like Moses, David, Job, John and Paul wrote stuff down as long as 4,000 years ago. There were no printers of course, so every copy of these prophetic words had to be hand written (or engraved) and were often not written down at all but transmitted orally (Citation for Oral Tradition, 2017). Naturally errors emerged over the centuries as mistakes were inadvertently generated or things were written based on someone's imperfect recollection. Additionally, others may have written things that were just plain false, like the news media often does today; I imagine they had 'fake news' too. Anyway, these records were floating around centuries ago when a group of leaders of what would become the Catholic Church of today, got together and decided what would and would not be included in this "Bible." You see, there were many, many books that 'might' have been scriptural, but only those that were voted "in" were included, based on the opinions of those involved and many New Testament texts were probably written after the first generation of church leaders were dead (Camille, 2017).

None of these scholars were of my specific faith, or yours, so can we really be certain that these guys included and rejected all the right records or even had all the records? Remember also that early Christians were persecuted for decades before the Catholic Church came to power. Do you suppose that the Romans did nothing to pervert the writings of the Christians (Ferguson, 2017)?

In fact, the Catholic Bible still has a number of books not included in most versions and there are also many more regarding New Testament Times that are not found in any Bible (Books of the Bible, 2017). One such book that is not found in any Bible, but is a possible gospel is known as the "Infancy" (of Christ) and among others, tells the story of the boy Jesus striking another boy dead and blinding his parents for bumping into Him (The Infancy Gospel of Thomas, 2017). Sound like inspired words to you? It didn't to the men who compiled the Bible either, but the decision on whether or not to include a particular book may have not always been so clear.

There are also others out there that seem to have been written by non-Christians attempting to thwart the faith or various writers that had a different perspective on things (see Ch.1: The Great Apostasy). The point here is that if you trust the Catholic scholars from centuries ago to have picked all the right books, rejected all the right books and even had all the right books to choose from, then you can maybe make a valid argument that the Bible is the complete and flawless word of God.

So, while the words of the prophets AS THEY WERE WRITTEN were most certainly inspired, we don't necessarily have those precise words. To say that the Bible is perfect (as we have it today) is to deny reality, but so also is it to say that it is unreliable. It is also a bit ironic to me that those that hold that the Bible is the infallible word of God assume flawless copies of each book of the Bible survived over the millennia as accurately as the day they were written and are rely on men of the past, with no particular prophetic calling to have compiled and translated this scripture with perfect accuracy. It also curious that everything God had to say for thousands of years can be covered in just over 1500 pages. By the way, that is only about 1 page every three years; perhaps God doesn't have much to say!

I cast my lot with Joseph Smith who said "I believe the Bible as it read when it came from the pen of the original writers. Ignorant translators, careless transcribers, or designing and corrupt priests have committed many errors" (Matthews, 1992).

Genesis 6:6

And GOD saw that the wickedness of man was great in the earth, and that every imagination of the thoughts of his heart was only evil continually. 6And it repented the LORD that he had made man on the earth, and it grieved him at his heart. 7And the LORD said, I will destroy man whom I have created from the face of the earth; both man, and beast, and the creeping thing, and the fowls of the air; for it repenteth me that I have made them.

I suspect that you already know that God does not need to repent, yet this verse and others like it throughout the Bible suggest that He does. Now, you might be saying to yourself "how does this prove anything? We all know that it doesn't really mean that God makes mistakes." But you see, that is precisely the point! This particular verse comes from the King James version of the Bible and there are others that use slightly different wording that does not suggest that God makes mistakes. Hence, which one is actually accurate? If the Bible is without error, which translation is infallible and why? They certainly all can't be given their differences, so what is there to suggest that this sort of "translation bias" never happened in the past when scripture was transcribed from copy to copy to copy an innumerable number of times before it made it to compilation?

Exodus 24: 6-7

6 And Moses took half of the blood, and put it in basons; and half of the blood he sprinkled on the altar.

7And he took the book of the covenant, and read in the audience of the people: and they said, All that the LORD hath said will we do, and be obedient.

So where is this "Book of the Covenant" that Moses apparently had? If Moses had it, it must be something inspired and thus scriptural, but why is it not found in the Bible? I suppose it could perhaps be a prayer book or something or it could be previous scripture written by an earlier prophet. In either case, why is it not found in the complete, flawless Bible?

Numbers 21:14

14Wherefore it is said in the book of the wars of the LORD, What he did in the Red sea, and in the brooks of Arnon,

Much like the last verse, we have reference to a book that does not appear to be in our modern Bible, yet its name denotes an inspired work. Admittedly however, it is not strong evidence, because it could be referring to accounts already found in the Old Testament and lumping them together in one term although it does specifically refer to it as a book.

Joshua 10:13

13And the sun stood still, and the moon stayed, until the people had avenged themselves upon their enemies. Is not this written in the book of Jasher? So the sun stood still in the midst of heaven, and hasted not to go down about a whole day.

This book actually does exist, but it is an Apocryphal work. It is in fact found in the Catholic Bible, but not in any other Protestant versions as there is doubt to its authenticity (Yee,

Gale A; Page Jr., Hugh R; Coomber, Matthew J.M., 2014). The fact that it is mentioned in the Bible as a source of prophecy strongly suggests that when Joshua wrote this, he had no doubt as to its inspired origin. So then why would it not be now? The answer of course is simple: over the centuries of copying and copying, things were changed and the Book of Jasher today is not the same as the day it was written.

1 Kings 11:41

41And the rest of the acts of Solomon, and all that he did, and his wisdom, are they not written in the book of the acts of Solomon?

So where is this book? Apparently lost. Now, I have to be objective here and admit that this book is mentioned immediately following a verse that tells us about Solomon trying to murder Jeroboam, so it is possible that the acts of Solomon weren't all that great and thus not inspired or scriptural. But it does further illustrate that things that were written then (even scripture) didn't necessarily make it to our day. If that is true, that not every shred of God-inspired writing survived thousands of years to make it into our modern-day Bible, we cannot fairly say that the Bible is complete.

1 Chronicles 29:29-30

29Now the acts of David the king, first and last, behold, they are written in the book of Samuel the seer, and in the book of Nathan the prophet, and in the book of Gad the seer,

30With all his reign and his might, and the times that went over him, and over Israel, and over all the kingdoms of the countries.

Wow, this is one of the best verses to support the premise that the Bible is NOT everything there is. The three men mentioned here are clearly men of God, and as such their acts must have been great and Godly. Yet there are no books by these names, but they must have been inspired and thus scriptural and certainly worthy of being included in a "Bible." So where are they? The fact that they are mentioned indicates that the author knew of their existence and had probably read them, but they all seem to have disappeared by the time the Bible was organized.

2 Chronicles 9:29

29 Now the rest of the acts of Solomon, first and last, are they not written in the book of Nathan the prophet, and in the prophecy of Ahijah the Shilonite, and in the visions of Iddo the seer against Jeroboam the son of Nebat?

So, Nathan and Ahijah were both prophets, Iddo was a seer, but their writings do not appear anywhere, yet there was clearly a book written on each one of them. There is no indication that these writings were biographies or auto-biographies, but in either case they were no doubt inspired as evidenced by the way in which they were presented in these verses.

2 Chronicles 12:15

15Now the acts of Rehoboam, first and last, are they not written in the book of Shemaiah the prophet, and of Iddo the seer concerning genealogies? And there were wars between Rehoboam and Jeroboam continually.

It seems from this verse and others that there were various prophets and men of God that we know absolutely nothing about because they are only mentioned in passing in the scripture that we do have. More than likely these men would have written something, or at least had someone write about what they did in the books that clearly were written, but they seemingly never made it to our time.

2 Chronicles 20:34

34Now the rest of the acts of Jehoshaphat, first and last, behold, they are written in the book of Jehu the son of Hanani, who is mentioned in the book of the kings of Israel.

The book of the Kings of Israel seems like it might be pretty important. Indisputably, the Bible contains much about some of those Kings, like David and Solomon, but certainly not all of them that ever existed. Where are these?

Matthew 27:5 vs. Acts 1:18

5 And he cast down the pieces of silver in the temple, and departed, and went and hanged himself.

18 Now this man purchased a field with the reward of iniquity; and falling headlong, he burst asunder in the midst, and all his bowels gushed out.

Now let me re-emphasize that I am not trying to suggest that the Bible is not scriptural or uninspired. I AM suggesting that it was scriptural and inspired when it was penned by its authors, but that changes have crept into the version we have today. These two scriptures are a prime example. While exactly how Judas killed himself may not be terribly important to anyone's salvation, these two accounts, both originally written by inspired men, differ quite significantly. St. Matthew says that Judas threw down the reward money for betraying Jesus and then went and hanged himself. The writer of Acts (probably Luke) writes that he took the blood money and bought a piece of land where he killed himself (but not necessary by hanging). So why the discrepancy? Being that both of these men were inspired men of God, my bet is that there was no discrepancy until through enough re-writings and translations, things got a little mixed up.

John 20:30, 21:25

30And many other signs truly did Jesus in the presence of his disciples, which are not written in this book:

25 And there are also many other things which Jesus did, the which, if they should be written every one, I suppose that even the world itself could not contain the books that should be written. Amen.

I included these verses together because they are basically saying the same thing, something that makes perfect sense, but is often overlooked by those whose knee-jerk reaction to the Bible is that it is flawless and complete. God is flawless and complete, but the Bible is not, partly because it can't possibly include everything that God has said and done through His prophets, as these verses indicate. Imagine someone following Jesus around recording everything He said and did. Just that alone would be a work far, FAR larger than our current Bible. Then imagine the same for all the prophets! We're talking libraries upon libraries of literature to cover the more than 4,000 years of events described in the Bible. Of course we don't have it all; how could we?

Ch. 3: Degrees of Glory

The standard Christian belief about ultimate destiny is that all men (and women too) either inherit everlasting happiness in heaven or eternal damnation in hell (Talbott, 2017). Now it seems pretty harsh to me that some dude that waved his hands in the air and "accepted Jesus" gets eternal bliss while another guy, who may actually be a "better person" rots in hell for eternity for failing to waive his hands in the air. I admit by saying this that I am being somewhat sarcastic and facetious, but I hope I make a point here. After all, the Bible says that we will be "…judged according to [our] works," (Rev. 20:12-13) which of course does not mean we are saved BECAUSE OF our works, but rather that our works are an outward expression of our love, faith and dedication to the Lord (see Ch.4: Faith and Works).

In the Mormon faith, we believe there are 3 degrees of glory for those that are faithful, all the way "down" to the murderers and rapists of the world. Yes, we believe in such an amazing, merciful and powerful Savior, who so desperately loves us, that even these piles of human trash will receive a level of glory, but then only after they suffer in Hell for an undetermined length of time (D&C 76).

Only those that deny the Holy Ghost (essentially spitting in God's face) will dwell with Satan forever. Now I'm not going to pretend that the Bible is clear on the matter, because it is not. However, there is strong Biblical evidence that there is not just a distinct Heaven and Hell, in much the same way that not everyone is fantastically rich or desperately poor.

John 14:2

2 In my Father's house are many mansions: if it were not so, I would have told you. I go to prepare a place for you.

At first it may not seem like this scripture proves anything at all, but by saying that there are "many" mansions, the Lord is implying there are "different" mansions. They may all be mansions, but they are not the same. Even if we believe in one Heaven, rather than degrees, this still suggests that we are all rewarded differently. Now if there is only one Heaven, then how could we all be rewarded differently? Granted, the argument is not very robust based on this scripture alone, but additional verses will tell us more.

1Corinthians 15:39-42

39 All flesh is not the same flesh: but there is one kind of flesh of men, another flesh of beasts, another of fishes, and another of birds.

40 There are also celestial bodies, and bodies terrestrial: but the glory of the celestial is one, and the glory of the terrestrial is another.

41 There is one glory of the sun, and another glory of the moon, and another glory of the stars: for one star differeth from another star in glory.

42 So also is the resurrection of the dead. It is sown in corruption; it is raised in incorruption:

Here Paul is speaking of the resurrection and he attempts to show that just like there are different kinds of "flesh," (birds, fish and people are not the same) those that are resurrected do not all experience the same glory. Some experience a glory comparable to the sun, others the moon and still others the stars. It might seem like a bit obscure of a scripture, but it is made quite clear in verse 42, after he has explained that there are 'different glories' that "so also is the resurrection."

2 Corinthians 12:2

14 2 I knew a man in Christ above fourteen years ago, (whether in the body, I cannot tell; or whether out of the body, I cannot tell: God knoweth;) such an one caught up to the third heaven.

Here's Paul again and this time he isn't really trying to teach us about degrees of glory and his reference to it is almost in passing. Apparently he met a man, but this man came to him in an experience that must have been a vision or at least vision-like, since he isn't even sure if he was 'in the body' at the time.

Now the more significant part is that this man was in 'the third Heaven.' Now why in the world would Paul distinguish between Heavens if there is only one? You wouldn't call your house your third house if you only owned one house. However, his comment matches perfectly with the idea of the existence of three degrees of glory because if you count from the bottom, the celestial kingdom (the "highest") is the third. Certainly, this isn't complete proof of the existence of three distinct "Heavens," but it no doubt implies more than one.

But wait a second, wouldn't God send a messenger from HIS glory, not from one of the "lower" glories? Then if there were, say 20 Heavens, would God send an angel from all the way "down" at the 3rd Heaven to speak with his mortal successor or one from the 20th heaven where He dwells?

Ch. 4: Faith and Works

The relationship amongst faith and works is exceedingly misunderstood by many Christians, but sometimes by us Mormons as well. Often we prefer to cite the Book of Mormon verse that reads "…for we know that it is by grace that we are saved, after all we can do" (2 Nephi 25:23) and conclude that in order to be saved we must work for our salvation and that Christ's sacrifice makes up for the portion we are unable to obtain by our own merits, when in reality our works are nothing more than an outward expression of our gratitude and faith and that our salvation comes *entirely* as a result of the atonement of Jesus Christ (conferencetalkabouthowHEpaysall). We can't even earn a portion of salvation on our own efforts, even if there were such a thing.

We home teach, visit teach, do family history, attend the temple, go to church for three hours every week, serve in the church with no pay, do community service, have lots of kids, and on and on. consequently, it is not difficult to imagine that someone not of our faith may infer that our intent is to *earn* our mansion on high. The reality is that the church doctrine on the subject is more similar to that of most Christians than it is different: Jesus Christ alone is our ticket to salvation and no work(s) we perform can move us closer to that goal. However, we also recognize that our works are meant to follow our faith and reflect our love of the Lord in the same way that a child "works" for his father for no other reason than to please him (McConkie, 1954). In other words, while our works do not save us, they do show that we are saved and that is precisely what the Bible teaches.

Matthew 7:21-27

21 Not every one that saith unto me, Lord, Lord, shall enter into the kingdom of heaven; but he that doeth the will of my Father which is in heaven.

22 Many will say to me in that day, Lord, Lord, have we not prophesied in thy name? and in thy name have cast out devils? and in thy name done many wonderful works?

23 And then will I profess unto them, I never knew you: depart from me, ye that work iniquity.

24 Therefore whosoever heareth these sayings of mine, and doeth them, I will liken him unto a wise man, which built his house upon a rock:

25 And the rain descended, and the floods came, and the winds blew, and beat upon that house; and it fell not: for it was founded upon a rock.

26 And every one that heareth these sayings of mine, and doeth them not, shall be likened unto a foolish man, which built his house upon the sand:

27 And the rain descended, and the floods came, and the winds blew, and beat upon that house; and it fell: and great was the fall of it.

Christ is quite clear in this passage by stating that only those that DO the will of his father will enter into the kingdom of heaven. The implication of course (if we take the entire Bible and gospel into correct context) is that the works themselves do not save, but the works are manifested by a true believer. In this scripture we are told of people who spoke and acted 'in Jesus' name,' but still remain unsaved. That is because they weren't doing His works, but really their own and by so doing are really rejecting the Lord.

Matthew 16:27

27 For the Son of man shall come in the glory of his Father with his angels; and then he shall reward every man according to his works.

Again, works are seemingly attached to rewards and this is sometimes where Mormons go wrong. There is no disputing here that men will be rewarded ACCORDING to their works, but not necessarily BECAUSE of them. As we will see through additional passages, the works do not merit the reward, but rather the works are an outward manifestation of faith and devotion.

Matthew 25:14-30

14 For the kingdom of heaven is as a man travelling into a far country, who called his own servants, and delivered unto them his goods.

15 And unto one he gave five talents, to another two, and to another one; to every man according to his several ability; and straightway took his journey.

16 Then he that had received the five talents went and traded with the same, and made them other five talents.

17 And likewise he that had received two, he also gained other two.

18 But he that had received one went and digged in the earth, and hid his lord's money.

19 After a long time the lord of those servants cometh, and reckoneth with them.

20 And so he that had received five talents came and brought other five talents, saying, Lord, thou deliveredst unto me five talents: behold, I have gained beside them five talents more.

21 His lord said unto him, Well done, thou good and faithful servant: thou hast been faithful over a few things, I will make thee ruler over many things: enter thou into the joy of thy lord.

22 He also that had received two talents came and said, Lord, thou deliveredst unto me two talents: behold, I have gained two other talents beside them.

23 His lord said unto him, Well done, good and faithful servant; thou hast been faithful over a few things, I will make thee ruler over many things: enter thou into the joy of thy lord.

24 Then he which had received the one talent came and said, Lord, I knew thee that thou art an hard man, reaping where thou hast not sown, and gathering where thou hast not strawed:

25 And I was afraid, and went and hid thy talent in the earth: lo, there thou hast that is thine.

26 His lord answered and said unto him, Thou wicked and slothful servant, thou knewest that I reap where I sowed not, and gather where I have not strawed:

27 Thou oughtest therefore to have put my money to the exchangers, and then at my coming I should have received mine own with usury.

28 Take therefore the talent from him, and give it unto him which hath ten talents.

29 For unto every one that hath shall be given, and he shall have abundance: but from him that hath not shall be taken away even that which he hath.

30 And cast ye the unprofitable servant into outer darkness: there shall be weeping and gnashing of teeth.

You are likely familiar with the parable of the talents already. As you will recall a talent refers to an ancient denomination of currency, although our modern definition of talent works quite well in this parable also (Elwell, Walter A; Comfort, Philip W;, 2001). Nonetheless, the essence of this narrative is that the "man" (Christ), gave his servants some money and expected them to DO something with it, namely generate a profit. Two of the servants accomplished precisely this objective, one more than the other, and both were rewarded accordingly. This shows how the atonement functions to save or "reward" all who receive a testimony and do something with it. Although one servant was given less than the other, he still DID what he could with it. The servant who DID nothing was condemned, as will we be if we know the truth and do nothing (or the wrong things) with that knowledge, in which case we are essentially rejecting Christ regardless of what we claim or say.

Luke 10:25-37

25 And, behold, a certain lawyer stood up, and tempted him, saying, Master, what shall I do to inherit eternal life?

26 He said unto him, What is written in the law? how readest thou?

27 And he answering said, Thou shalt love the Lord thy God with all thy heart, and with all thy soul, and with all thy strength, and with all thy mind; and thy neighbour as thyself.

28 And he said unto him, Thou hast answered right: this do, and thou shalt live.

29 But he, willing to justify himself, said unto Jesus, And who is my neighbour?

30 And Jesus answering said, A certain man went down from Jerusalem to Jericho, and fell among thieves, which stripped him of his raiment, and wounded him, and departed, leaving him half dead.

31 And by chance there came down a certain priest that way: and when he saw him, he passed by on the other side.

32 And likewise a Levite, when he was at the place, came and looked on him, and passed by on the other side.

33 But a certain Samaritan, as he journeyed, came where he was: and when he saw him, he had compassion on him,

34 And went to him, and bound up his wounds, pouring in oil and wine, and set him on his own beast, and brought him to an inn, and took care of him.

35 And on the morrow when he departed, he took out two pence, and gave them to the host, and said unto him, Take care of him; and whatsoever thou spendest more, when I come again, I will repay thee.

36 Which now of these three, thinkest thou, was neighbour unto him that fell among the thieves?

37 And he said, He that shewed mercy on him. Then said Jesus unto him, Go, and do thou likewise.

Here again Christ employs an anecdote to illustrate the relationship between faith and works, this time with a Jew and a Samaritan. In the days of Christ these two groups despised one another and would commonly travel much farther than necessary merely to avoid interaction (Haddad, 2016). Thus, there is particular significance in the story of Samaritan helping a Jew, especially when so-called "holy men" chose to ignore him.

The works portion of this incident is fairly obvious because the Samaritan DID something, like the two servants in the Parable of the Talents. However, it also illustrates further that simply believing is insufficient. It can reasonably be assumed that the priest and the Levite, both of whom would have been considered religious in their time, actually believed in God, but failed to show it and thus in some sense are in fact rejecting Him.

John 5:28-29

28 Marvel not at this: for the hour is coming, in the which all that are in the graves shall hear his voice,

29 And shall come forth; they that have done good, unto the resurrection of life; and they that have done evil, unto the resurrection of damnation.

If ever there were a scripture that indisputably illustrates the relationship between faith and works, this is it. In fact, verse 29 seems to imply that works are the one factor determining salvation by declaring that do-gooders will get be resurrected unto "life." We know that the only real factor determining salvation is Jesus Christ, but that works will follow true faith. So, although works do not technically save us, they are so integral to true belief in Jesus Christ that John can accurately state that "they that have DONE good unto the resurrection of life; and they that have done evil [works] unto...damnation" (emphasis added).

John 14:12

12 Verily, verily, I say unto you, He that believeth on me, the works that I do shall he do also; and greater works than these shall he do; because I go unto my Father.

This scripture quite elegantly places the previous ones, some seemingly only concerned with works, in context. Christ himself suggests that the true believer will perform greater works that even He has. This theoretical believer that the Savior refers to accomplishes these works precisely because of his belief. In modern Christian terms, this man has been "saved" and as a result, his works follow, not the other way around; we are not saved because of our works, we are saved and then we want to work.

Acts 16:29-34

29 Then he called for a light, and sprang in, and came trembling, and fell down before Paul and Silas,

30 And brought them out, and said, Sirs, what must I do to be saved?

31 And they said, Believe on the Lord Jesus Christ, and thou shalt be saved, and thy house.

32 And they spake unto him the word of the Lord, and to all that were in his house.

33 And he took them the same hour of the night, and washed their stripes; and was baptized, he and all his, straightway.

34 And when he had brought them into his house, he set meat before them, and rejoiced, believing in God with all his house.

This is yet another Bible passage that shows men "working" for the Lord, but here we see what a believer is to DO when they find the truth. When the jailor is converted by Paul and Silas he clearly did not wave his hands in the air and simply accept Jesus into his heart (which would be DOING something by the way), instead he went home and was baptized with his household. He was baptized because that is what the Lord asks us to do, not because baptism in itself has some magical property of salvation, but because when we are converted we DO what the Lord asks.

Romans 2:5-10, 23

5 But after thy hardness and impenitent heart treasurest up unto thyself wrath against the day of wrath and revelation of the righteous judgment of God;

6 Who will render to every man according to his deeds:

7 To them who by patient continuance in well doing seek for glory and honour and immortality, eternal life:

8 But unto them that are contentious, and do not obey the truth, but obey unrighteousness, indignation and wrath,

9 Tribulation and anguish, upon every soul of man that doeth evil, of the Jew first, and also of the Gentile;

10 But glory, honour, and peace, to every man that worketh good, to the Jew first, and also to the Gentile:

23 Thou that makest thy boast of the law, through breaking the law dishonourest thou God?

This scripture is very clear with the fact that those that do good are those that will be saved. Those who do not will be damned. Therefore, one must "work" to be saved, not because works save them, but because good works will naturally spring forth from true conversion.

1 Corinthians 3:8

7 So then neither is he that planteth any thing, neither he that watereth; but God that giveth the increase.

8 Now he that planteth and he that watereth are one: and every man shall receive his own reward according to his own labour.

Here Paul compares us to those that plant and water. He provides an interesting insight by suggesting that we are not "any thing," in other words our efforts are insignificant compared to God's, but that our efforts (works) determine our eternal reward. So even though our contribution to our own salvation is a big fat zero, the Lord expects us to work for that zero.

2 Corinthians 5:10

9 Wherefore we labour, that, whether present or absent, we may be accepted of him.

10 For we must all appear before the judgment seat of Christ; that every one may receive the things done in his body, according to that he hath done, whether it be good or bad.

Again, the idea here is that we are "accepted" by God according to our works and that at the judgment Christ will judge us based on the things we have done. In other words, have we shown by what we did that we accepted Him as our Savior and King or did we just pay lip-service to the idea?

Galatians 5: 19-21

19 Now the works of the flesh are manifest, which are these; Adultery, fornication, uncleanness, lasciviousness,

20 Idolatry, witchcraft, hatred, variance, emulations, wrath, strife, seditions, heresies,

21 Envyings, murders, drunkenness, revellings, and such like: of the which I tell you before, as I have also told you in time past, that they which do such things shall not inherit the kingdom of God.

Even if there were a convincing argument that waving your hands in the air and asking Jesus to save your soul was all that had to be done to obtain eternal glory, this verse makes it clear your works can and WILL affect your salvation; If you DO anything in this list, you will

NOT inherit the kingdom of God. Of course, there are an abundance of individuals that have committed one or more of these offenses and repented; there are plenty of scriptural and modern-day examples. These people are not forever condemned based on past crimes, those who are condemned here are ones who DO these things and DO NOT repent. They choose by their works to reject the truth rather than to "work" to accept it.

Ephesians 2:8-10

8 For by grace are ye saved through faith; and that not of yourselves: it is the gift of God:

9 Not of works, lest any man should boast.

10 For we are his workmanship, created in Christ Jesus unto good works, which God hath before ordained that we should walk in them.

This is one of the best Bible scriptures for explaining the proper role between faith and works. Some Christians so-called prefer to read the first part about how grace comes through faith and "…Not of works," while ignoring the remainder of the verse. It is true that grace comes only through faith, there is nothing we can do to earn it, but God "…created [us] in Christ Jesus unto good works." In other words, God created us with the purpose of DOING good works, which we will if we are truly converted and truly saved.

Philippians 2:12-15

12 Wherefore, my beloved, as ye have always obeyed, not as in my presence only, but now much more in my absence, work out your own salvation with fear and trembling.

13 For it is God which worketh in you both to will and to do of his good pleasure.

14 Do all things without murmurings and disputings:

15 That ye may be blameless and harmless, the sons of God, without rebuke, in the midst of a crooked and perverse nation, among whom ye shine as lights in the world;

We can agree with our Christian friends that salvation only comes through Jesus Christ and faith in Him, but if this is true why would Paul suggest that his brethren "…do…things" if all we have to do is believe? It doesn't make much sense unless those that display righteous works are the people that have already truly accepted Christ and received of His grace; in the words of Christendom, "been saved."

1 Thessalonians 1:7-9

7 And to you who are troubled rest with us, when the Lord Jesus shall be revealed from heaven with his mighty angels,

8 In flaming fire taking vengeance on them that know not God, and that obey not the gospel of our Lord Jesus Christ:

9 Who shall be punished with everlasting destruction from the presence of the Lord, and from the glory of his power;

Paul illustrates the unsettling fate of those that reject the Lord because they "…obey not the gospel of our Lord Jesus Christ." In other words, they do NOT DO the gospel. Obeying is a work and if we don't do it, we will suffer, not because of our failure to earn salvation, but because our obedience (works) reflect our faithfulness.

2 Timothy 3:16-17

16 All scripture is given by inspiration of God, and is profitable for doctrine, for reproof, for correction, for instruction in righteousness:

17 That the man of God may be perfect, throughly furnished unto all good works.

You may notice a couple of things in this scripture that are significant in terms of works as they relate to the gospel and salvation. First of all, it states that scripture is profitable for several things including "instruction in righteousness." The term righteousness strongly suggest works, but it is clearer when you read verse 17, which essentially says that God wants us to perform good works. And why not, wasn't Christ's entire life a series of good works?

Titus 3:8

8 This is a faithful saying, and these things I will that thou affirm constantly, that they which have believed in God might be careful to maintain good works. These things are good and profitable unto men.

The significance of this verse is the clear path that the gospel represents. First a person believes and then they "maintain good works." Although a little off the subject of this chapter, being as Paul says that believers need to maintain good works, the implication is that a believer can fall away or "backslide" by not doing good deeds.

James 2:14-26

14 What doth it profit, my brethren, though a man say he hath faith, and have not works? can faith save him?

15 If a brother or sister be naked, and destitute of daily food,

16 And one of you say unto them, Depart in peace, be ye warmed and filled; notwithstanding ye give them not those things which are needful to the body; what doth it profit?

17 Even so faith, if it hath not works, is dead, being alone.

18 Yea, a man may say, Thou hast faith, and I have works: shew me thy faith without thy works, and I will shew thee my faith by my works.

19 Thou believest that there is one God; thou doest well: the devils also believe, and tremble.

20 But wilt thou know, O vain man, that faith without works is dead?

21 Was not Abraham our father justified by works, when he had offered Isaac his son upon the altar?

22 Seest thou how faith wrought with his works, and by works was faith made perfect?

23 And the scripture was fulfilled which saith, Abraham believed God, and it was imputed unto him for righteousness: and he was called the Friend of God.

24 Ye see then how that by works a man is justified, and not by faith only.

25 Likewise also was not Rahab the harlot justified by works, when she had received the messengers, and had sent them out another way?

26 For as the body without the spirit is dead, so faith without works is dead also.

This is a particularly clear passage that illustrates the role of works and its relationship to the Plan of Salvation. The story about the neighbor that is "…naked and destitute…" uses common sense to drive home the point that just having good intentions, or faith without works, is insufficient. Only by actually clothing and feeding the neighbor is righteousness accomplished. Within these verses is also a powerful counter to the "just believe to be saved" crowd where Paul says that even the Devil "believes," but we can all agree that he is not and will not ever be saved. Clearly works are an important distinguishing factor between the true believers and those that believe but produce no works of righteousness. As if this is not enough evidence of the role of works in the plan of salvation, the repeated use of the words "faith without works is dead" makes it even more undisputable.

James 4:17

17 Therefore to him that knoweth to do good, and doeth it not, to him it is sin.

The clear explanation here is that if you know to DO good and don't, you are sinning. So not only is faith manifest in works, lack of faith is manifested in lack of works.

2 Peter 2:20-22

20 For if after they have escaped the pollutions of the world through the knowledge of the Lord and Savior Jesus Christ, they are again entangled therein, and overcome, the latter end is worse with them than the beginning.

21 For it had been better for them not to have known the way of righteousness, than, after they have known it, to turn from the holy commandment delivered unto them.

22 But it is happened unto them according to the true proverb, The dog is turned to his own vomit again; and the sow that was washed to her wallowing in the mire.

There is very little left to interpretation in these verses, but its relation to works is a little deeper, more of an implication. Essentially Peter is warning those that have already obtained a "knowledge of the Lord and Savior Jesus Christ" and turned from it. This clearly flies in the face of the doctrine of once saved always saved, but also relates to the works of that person. Since it states that this person was already familiar with the commandments (which all require works) and turned from them, this implies that this individual was "working" righteousness and no longer is. Thus, righteousness requires good works.

1 John 2:3-6

3 And hereby we do know that we know him, if we keep his commandments.

4 He that saith, I know him, and keepeth not his commandments, is a liar, and the truth is not in him.

5 But whoso keepeth his word, in him verily is the love of God perfected: hereby know we that we are in him.

6 He that saith he abideth in him ought himself also so to walk, even as he walked.

There are two parts to this passage, both of which concern works, but in different aspects. First of all, John makes it clear in verse 3 that we can be sure we know Jesus if we keep his commandments (not just believe in Him). Certainly, keeping the commandments of God requires works. Second, John states that the person that claims to believe in Christ needs to "…walk, even as he walked," meaning to do the works He did.

Revelations 2:23

23 And I will kill her children with death; and all the churches shall know that I am he which searcheth the reins and hearts: and I will give unto every one of you according to your works.

This is one of the more brutal-sounding New Testament scriptures in which the Lord warns against falling away from the Gospel. He parses no words here; He will assign rewards/punishments ACCORDING to works.

Revelation 20:12-13

12 And I saw the dead, small and great, stand before God; and the books were opened: and another book was opened, which is the bookof life: and the dead were judged out of those things which were written in the books, according to their works.

13 And the sea gave up the dead which were in it; and death and hell delivered up the dead which were in them: and they were judged every man according to their works.

It is succinctly stated in this passage (twice) that we will stand before God to be judged 'according to our works.' Now this scripture almost sounds like our works are what determine our fate. We already know from other scriptures and the Gospel that Christ is the only one that can save and that works follow conversion, but just try to let your "saved" friends explain this one in a meaningful way that DOESN'T include the necessity of works!

Revelation 22:12-13

12 And, behold, I come quickly; and my reward is with me, to give every man according as his work shall be.

13 I am Alpha and Omega, the beginning and the end, the first and the last.

14 Blessed are they that do his commandments, that they may have right to the tree of life, and may enter in through the gates into the city.

If you have read the other scriptures in this chapter then this passage requires little explanation. As with others, God is stating that works are attached to salvation, which implies that belief alone is not sufficient. Remember, even the Devil believes, but his works clearly do not imply devotion to God.

Ch. 5: Godhood

This is a difficult topic that is really tough for people to grasp outside of the Church of Jesus Christ because the knee-jerk response from most Christians is offense that we think ourselves equal to God. I would be offended too if someone thought themselves equal to God, but that is not what we in fact believe. We don't imagine we are equal to God, or that we ever will be, but that He can and will elevate us to what He is in much the same way that a son is "elevated" to become a father with the help of that father (D&C 132:19-20).

Sometimes we Mormons sort of cower away from this idea in mixed company because the standard Christian philosophy is that we go to Heaven or Hell when we die and just exist there for all eternity doing whatever it is angels (or demons) do, but that's where almost all Christian denominations stop. In fact, they often don't even profess to know what it is we do besides praise God; anything else is just speculation (Kreeft, 2017). Mormons on the other hand believe that death is just the beginning of an eternity of learning and progressing (Preparing for Eternal Progression, 1997). Most other Christians however just can't swallow the idea of being like God, but the very Bible they use is by no means silent on the subject, but seeing it takes much more thought than just skimming through the scriptures.

But before we dive into the Bible on this subject, let me share a purely rational, logical explanation, based on the entirety of the Biblical scriptures that will be presented shortly, as to why NOT having the option of becoming like God is a nonsensical idea . Few will disagree that God is all powerful, meaning He can do *anything;* of course there are many things He won't do, but He could. If this is true, He must then have the power to make us into all-knowing gods if He wanted to. To say He cannot is to say the He is NOT all powerful. Since He certainly CAN do this, why would He not? No doubt His existence is superior to ours, so why then would He not want for us what He has? I can't think of a single reason (maybe you can) that He would not do something that would magnify our existence if He could. To suggest so would be to insinuate that He does not want the absolute best for us, just himself. Surely this is not the God of the Bible. Or perhaps some of us might "turn" on him with our new-found power, but of course this is tantamount to saying that God is NOT all-knowing if He is unsure who would use their power for evil.

The point is, there is no surprise that the concept of becoming just like God (someday; probably far, FAR, FAR in the future) is instantaneously rejected by the non-Mormon Christian world, but I have yet to hear a single reasonable or Biblical argument to its opposition.

Psalm 82:5-7

5 They know not, neither will they understand; they walk on in darkness: all the foundations of the earth are out of course.

6 I have said, Ye are gods; and all of you are children of the most High.

7 But ye shall die like men, and fall like one of the princes.

This Psalm is essentially a warning to unbelievers stating that although they "are gods," they shall perish like other men and fall like a prince (probably a reference to Satan) if they don't follow the God of Heaven. The noteworthy part here is that these "men" are referred to as "gods," not for some obscure reason such as a mistranslation of the Greek or as an analogous reference, but because those men have the potential to be as God is. As with other chapters, this scripture alone certainly does not prove my point, but it does provide evidence that this and the following scriptures are indeed suggesting that our potential is as infinite as God.

Matthew 5:48

48 Be ye therefore perfect, even as your Father which is in heaven is perfect.

Jesus commands us to be perfect and therefore so does God. But how are we to be perfect? As far as we know only one man has ever lived a perfect life and that was Jesus Christ. Yet God commands us to be perfect. I don't suppose any reader would suggest that this is possible, at least in this life, so why would Jesus command us to do something if accomplishment is impossible. I would suggest that the reason is not because we even can be perfect in this life, but perfection is what we should be striving for because that is God's plan ultimate plan is for us.

Christians everywhere believe that Christ paid for our sins. In fact, one can hardly argue against the idea that this is sort of the definition of Christianity. So then, if we have no sin because Jesus paid the price, are we not then perfect? Is being sinless not the very definition of perfection? If we are then perfect, why are we (spiritually) any different from God himself?

John 10:30-35

31 Then the Jews took up stones again to stone him.

32 Jesus answered them, Many good works have I shewed you from my Father; for which of those works do ye stone me?

33 The Jews answered him, saying, For a good work we stone thee not; but for blasphemy; and because that thou, being a man, makest thyself God.

34 Jesus answered them, Is it not written in your law, I said, Ye are gods?

35 If he called them gods, unto whom the word of God came, and the scripture cannot be broken;

The Jews get really angry at Jesus here, despite all of His good works, because He is essentially calling himself God, which Obviously He is. But in their minds He is just a man and so wish to stone Him for blasphemy. Then He asks them if it is not written in their law (perhaps Psalm 82) that "[they] are gods." This naturally is a rhetorical question and Jesus knows quite well that their law (or the scriptures of the time) does say that, even though they don't understand it. The point here is not so much that Jesus is calling himself God but that He is stating that men are potential gods as stated in the scriptures.

Romans 8:16-17

16 The Spirit itself beareth witness with our spirit, that we are the children of God:

17 And if children, then heirs; heirs of God, and joint-heirs with Christ; if so be that we suffer with him, that we may be also glorified together.

Paul doesn't parse words here in making it clear that we are joint heirs with Christ. But here's the secret; no matter how many heirs God has, they are all capable of receiving all things. This based on a simple mathematical principle of infinity. Infinity is what God has and if you split infinity into two parts, both are infinite. If you split it into an infinite number of parts, each part is still infinite; unlike the concept of joint heirs in our world in which the total is divided into smaller finite parts based on the number of inheritors.

Now remember, we are joint-heirs with Christ, which of course means that we will inherit all He has which must therefore include all knowledge. Someday we will return to the presence of God through the blood of Christ, and if He were to teach us all things (so that we became all-knowing and therefore all-powerful), God would not have given up anything, but we would have received all knowledge from Him as has Christ. So, if we are sinless through Christ's blood and are taught "all things," aren't we then gods (although I did not say equal to God).

1 Corinthians 6:2-3

2 Do ye not know that the saints shall judge the world? and if the world shall be judged by you, are ye unworthy to judge the smallest matters?

3 Know ye not that we shall judge angels? how much more things that pertain to this life?

Paul's letter to the Corinthians includes these verses and others in which he is explaining that the saints should take their disagreements before the church, not the law. To get his point across he says that the saints will judge the world, so why can't they work out their comparatively petty differences within the church. After all, these are far less important than judging the world. But he takes his point one step further with another rhetorical question that asks why they can't judge the things of this world when they will be judging angels. Well who judges angels? Apparently the saints do according to Paul, but when will that happen? Certainly not in this life, but what about the next life when we are as gods. Will we judge angels when we ourselves are angels? That just doesn't make sense. If we are above the angels, as gods, that would seem to be the only logical reason for us to "judge" angels.

Galatians 4:7

7 Wherefore thou art no more a servant, but a son; and if a son, then an heir of God through Christ.

We have previously discussed the significance of being an heir of God and joint heir with Christ, which can only reasonably mean that God will give us all that He has, which is everything; all knowledge and therefore all power. Don't mistake this for glory however. We will never be "equal" with God given that He got started LONG before us and is already ahead of us in 'glory collection,' so to speak. Nonetheless, there is no reasonable explanation for why God would not make us into what He is, especially considering this verse, Romans 8 and (later) Hebrews 1, which make it abundantly clear that we are heir to ALL things as joint heirs of Christ.

2 Timothy 2:7:10-12

10 Therefore I endure all things for the elect's sakes, that they may also obtain the salvation which is in Christ Jesus with eternal glory.

11 It is a faithful saying: For if we be dead with him, we shall also live with him:

12 If we suffer, we shall also reign with him: if we deny him, he also will deny us:

Paul here is explaining to Timothy, the bishop of the Ephesian church that the reason he is laboring and enduring through all the persecution he is experiencing is to help others obtain salvation through Christ. He explains further that if we endure in Christ we will be with Him, but that we will also reign with Him. Paul did not say reign under Him or watch Him reign, but reign WITH Him.

The funny thing is that this passage, as with so many others, would arguably be more poignant if the Trinity were indeed three beings in one as most of Christendom holds because in that case Jesus is God and we would therefore be reigning with God. Without doubt, this is not true (see Ch.9: The Trinity), but even then the scripture makes it clear that we will reign with Christ, who we Mormons know to be the son of God and as the Bible clearly states, heir of all things.

Hebrews 1:1-2

1 God, who at sundry times and in divers manners spake in time past unto the fathers by the prophets,

2 Hath in these last days spoken unto us by his Son, whom he hath appointed heir of all things, by whom also he made the worlds;

I promised to share a scripture that went along well with Romans 8 and this is it. Paul is very precise here in stating that Christ is "heir of all things." Thus whether or not you believe in the Trinity or separate members of the Godhead, it is clear from this statement that whoever Christ is, He will inherit ALL things. Now remember, Romans and Galatians taught us that we are joint heirs with Christ. Thus, by definition, we are also heir of all things. Perhaps worth noting too is that Paul states here that Christ made the worlds. Of course, we already knew that and it is hardly a disputed doctrine in most denominations, but it is interesting to note that Christ created the worlds (plural by the way) BEFORE He obtained all things.

Ch. 6: Plural Marriage

The topic of polygamy is a touchy one. When we discuss it with people, we Mormons tend to relay what I call it's "excuses". We talk about how only a couple percent of members practiced it, the prophet had to call you to be part of it, and of course we no longer practice it, almost as if it were a mistake. We also make a distinction between us and fringe (former) Mormons that still practice polygamy; they are bad and we are good.

But the fact of the matter is that plural marriage is a Celestial law, evidenced by the fact that even today, a man may be sealed to a second, third, etc. wife after the former dies (or even divorced civilly), and although the realities regarding the early church's practice of polygamy are important, no excuse need be made for the practice. For God commanded polygamy to start and God commanded it to stop (Plural Marriage in The Church of Jesus Christ of Latter-day Saints, 2017). In fact, God himself may have many wives, although that is only speculation since we are told that the practice of polygamy is not necessary for salvation but is to be practiced only at God's command through the prophet of the day (Nash, 2015).

Nevertheless, polygamy has been practiced almost since the beginning of time because it was first instituted by God and having only one wife is a historically recent ideal of Western civilization; even today many cultures practice it (Ghose, 2013) (Vallely, 2010). Please don't misunderstand me. I am not suggesting that polygamy is justified in the fact that it is historically widespread, but that it is historically widespread because it originated with the gospel.

In the Bible as well, it has been practiced by mighty men of God as it was practiced in the early days of the church by more recent mighty men of God. Ironically, the Book of Mormon says very little on the subject other than a condemnation for its practice by a people that were

NOT doing it because God commanded so and further states that if the Lord commands men to have more than one wife, then that is what they should do; emphasis on "IF" (Jacob 2:21).

The New Testament is quite scarce on the subject as well, but it does exemplify the prophets of the Old Testament who DID practice polygamy. Israel had several wives who birthed the men that would later become the Twelve Tribes. David was "given" many wives by the Lord, but later when he turned to 'the dark side' he was condemned for taking on more wives because they Lord did not command it (2 Samuel 12:8). All throughout the majority of Biblical history, polygamy has been practiced. It is really only in the last few hundred years that we have decided (as a society) that it is wrong, which is patently true if God has not commanded it. So, either the old prophets (who spoke to God by the way) were incredibly naive, the laws of God change with the times or polygamy is in fact a higher order law.

Genesis 16:1-11

1 Now Sarai Abram's wife bare him no children: and she had an handmaid, an Egyptian, whose name was Hagar.

2 And Sarai said unto Abram, Behold now, the LORD hath restrained me from bearing: I pray thee, go in unto my maid; it may be that I may obtain children by her. And Abram hearkened to the voice of Sarai.

3 And Sarai Abram's wife took Hagar her maid the Egyptian, after Abram had dwelt ten years in the land of Canaan, and gave her to her husband Abram to be his wife.

4 And he went in unto Hagar, and she conceived: and when she saw that she had conceived, her mistress was despised in her eyes.

5 And Sarai said unto Abram, My wrong be upon thee: I have given my maid into thy bosom; and when she saw that she had conceived, I was despised in her eyes: the LORD judge between me and thee.

6 But Abram said unto Sarai, Behold, thy maid is in thy hand; do to her as it pleaseth thee. And when Sarai dealt hardly with her, she fled from her face.

7 And the angel of the LORD found her by a fountain of water in the wilderness, by the fountain in the way to Shur.

8 And he said, Hagar, Sarai's maid, whence camest thou? and whither wilt thou go? And she said, I flee from the face of my mistress Sarai.

9 And the angel of the LORD said unto her, Return to thy mistress, and submit thyself under her hands.

10 And the angel of the LORD said unto her, I will multiply thy seed exceedingly, that it shall not be numbered for multitude.

11 And the angel of the LORD said unto her, Behold, thou art with child, and shalt bear a son, and shalt call his name Ishmael; because the LORD hath heard thy affliction.

The common defense I have heard repeated many times by non-Mormons for why plural marriage was "allowed" in the old testament amounts to a lack of understanding by those that practiced it. It is quite strange to think that men who literally walked and talked with God would not understand or not know any better and yet the common Christian of our day who has NOT walked and talked with God.

It is even more curious that the "gospel" of the New Testament, as interpreted again by non-Mormons, suggests that plural marriage is akin to adultery, but the Old Law defines it as perfectly acceptable, and even commanded by God as is clearly stated by His sanction of it in these verses. In this chapter Abraham takes Hagar, his wife's handmaid to wife, which at first may seem like only a "convenient" situation given that Sarai could not bear children and *that she requested it.*[1] Sarai eventually becomes jealous when Hagar ends up pregnant and sends her away. But something interesting happens; the angel of God appears to Hagar and tells her to go back and promises her to "multiply [her] seed" and even tells her what to name her son. The point here is that God is clearly behind all of this and not only approves, but it is part of His plan. As the story progresses we find that Ishmael becomes a major player in Biblical history and had it not been for the marriage of Abraham and Hagar, he presumably never would have been born.

Genesis 17:1-8

1 And when Abram was ninety years old and nine, the LORD appeared to Abram, and said unto him, I am the Almighty God; walk before me, and be thou perfect.

2 And I will make my covenant between me and thee, and will multiply thee exceedingly.

3 And Abram fell on his face: and God talked with him, saying,

4 As for me, behold, my covenant is with thee, and thou shalt be a father of many nations.

5 Neither shall thy name any more be called Abram, but thy name shall be Abraham; for a father of many nations have I made thee.

6 And I will make thee exceeding fruitful, and I will make nations of thee, and kings shall come out of thee.

---

[1] In the early days of the Church of Jesus Christ of Latter-day Saints when polygamy was practiced, the "primary" wife was an active part of the choosing of additional wives in the same tradition of these verses.

7 And I will establish my covenant between me and thee and thy seed after thee in their generations for an everlasting covenant, to be a God unto thee, and to thy seed after thee.

8 And I will give unto thee, and to thy seed after thee, the land wherein thou art a stranger, all the land of Canaan, for an everlasting possession; and I will be their God.

The passages here are a continuation of the previous narrative. To review, Abram took on a second wife, Hagar, and through her Ishmael was born and God clearly sanctified the union. Here again God emphasizes His approval of Abram (now Abraham), not in spite of his additional wife, but because he obeyed God in taking her on. Not only does God appear to him, but He also covenants with Abraham to make him a "father of many nations." Consequently, unless God "overlooked" adultery, adultery suddenly went from good to bad in the New Testament, or Abraham was just clueless, God clearly gave him more than one wife.

2 Samuel 2:1-2

1 And it came to pass after this, that David enquired of the LORD, saying, Shall I go up into any of the cities of Judah? And the LORD said unto him, Go up. And David said, Whither shall I go up? And he said, Unto Hebron.

2 So David went up thither, and his two wives also, Ahinoam the Jezreelitess, and Abigail Nabal's wife the Carmelite.

David was justified in his taking on multiple wives in the same way in which Abraham was previously. This may seem like a filler scripture simply regarding David's travels with his two wives, but if we read between the lines we realize that God was with him. He prayed to God to ask where to go and God answered that he should go to Hebron. If David were committing adultery God certainly would not be guiding him and yet He does exactly that.

2 Samuel 12:7-8

7 And Nathan said to David, Thou art the man. Thus saith the LORD God of Israel, I anointed thee king over Israel, and I delivered thee out of the hand of Saul;

8 And I gave thee thy master's house, and thy master's wives into thy bosom, and gave thee the house of Israel and of Judah; and if that had been too little, I would moreover have given unto thee such and such things.

After David took Bathsheba and made sure her husband was killed in the war, the Lord condemned him through the prophet Nathan. The Lord reminds David that He protected him from Saul and that He (the Lord) made David king. The most relevant part to our discussion in this chapter is the Lord's reminder that *He gave David his house and his wives*. By this time David had many wives, but the Lord clearly states that HE gave them to David.

Isaiah 4:1-2

1 And in that day seven women shall take hold of one man, saying, We will eat our own bread, and wear our own apparel: only let us be called by thy name, to take away our reproach.

2 In that day shall the branch of the LORD be beautiful and glorious, and the fruit of the earth shall be excellent and comely for them that are escaped of Israel.

The words of Isaiah can be difficult to understand, but if we look at what is being said here, we can see some implication of God's acceptance of plural marriage in the last days. First it says that at some point there will be about seven women for every man and that the women will all beg men to marry them to "take away their reproach." Now this may not seem like a strong scripture supporting plural marriage until you consider who these women are. Isaiah is

NOT speaking of the wicked, but the righteous. This must be the case because the word "reproach" indicates that these particular women don't want the stigma of being unmarried and childless. If that is true then they must be saints since being married and having children are usually not high priorities for the wicked.

Further, since these are faithful women, it would figure that they would only marry men seven at a time if God had authorized such. If plural marriage is indeed always "wrong" (according to mainstream Christianity), why in the last days would faithful women engage in plural marriage?

Matthew 8:11, Luke 13:28, 16:23-24

11 And I say unto you, That many shall come from the east and west, and shall sit down with Abraham, and Isaac, and Jacob, in the kingdom of heaven.

28 There shall be weeping and gnashing of teeth, when ye shall see Abraham, and Isaac, and Jacob, and all the prophets, in the kingdom of God, and you yourselves thrust out.

23 And in hell he lift up his eyes, being in torments, and seeth Abraham afar off, and Lazarus in his bosom.

24 And he cried and said, Father Abraham, have mercy on me, and send Lazarus, that he may dip the tip of his finger in water, and cool my tongue; for I am tormented in this flame.

Jesus makes it clear in these passages that Abraham, Isaac and Jacob "made it" so to speak; They will be in heaven with God. They all had multiple wives and in fact the very Children of Israel sprang from Jacob (Israel) as a result of plural marriage. Therefore, as we have discussed already, unless polygamy was somehow acceptable in the Old Testament, but not in the New (which would require God to change) or these great prophets just 'didn't understand' (which would require these PROPHETS to understand less than the average Christian of today), then God intended for them to have multiple wives.

Ch. 7: The Premortal Existence

I don't speak for other religions, but in my interactions with those of other faiths, most seem to never have really thought about whether or not they existed before conception. From a doctrinal perspective, some Christian religions and individuals do believe in some sort of existence prior to mortal life, but it seems that most do not; many believing that a person, although eternal, comes into existence sometime between conception and birth (Comparison of Christian Religions, 2017).

Anyone familiar with the Mormon faith knows that the premortal existence is a fundamental doctrine for us, although even members do not grasp the details. We actually believe that we have existed in some form or another for all eternity, just as God, but as something referred to as "intelligence." (D&C 93) Whatever this is has not been entirely revealed, but it is apparently what God "uses" to create spirits (you and I) that ultimately inhabit bodies and head along the path we are on. My personal view is that intelligence is something that we cannot comprehend because it is not an actual "thing." I think it is the potential for spirit, much like a man and a woman are potential parents. It's not as if they have to make anything to give life to a child, just as I don't think God is fashioning some sort of ethereal clay into spirit. If he were, it would imply that there is something "beyond" him; that an all-knowing, all-powerful God has to rely on some sort of "stuff" to create spirit children.

Anyway, enough of my thoughts, they are largely speculation anyway because we just don't have the whole story, and that's fine. But what we do have is evidence all throughout scripture that we lived with God before we were born.

Job 38: 1-7

1 Then the LORD answered Job out of the whirlwind, and said,

2 Who is this that darkeneth counsel by words without knowledge?

3 Gird up now thy loins like a man; for I will demand of thee, and answer thou me.

4 Where wast thou when I laid the foundations of the earth? declare, if thou hast understanding.

5 Who hath laid the measures thereof, if thou knowest? or who hath stretched the line upon it?

6 Whereupon are the foundations thereof fastened? or who laid the corner stone thereof;

7 When the morning stars sang together, and all the sons of God shouted for joy?

It is quite clear from verse 1 that God is speaking to Job. He then asks some questions, amounting to 'where were you when I created the earth?' However, in verse 7, the Lord's question includes the phrase "…and all the sons of God shouted for joy." Now how could the sons of God shout for joy at the creation of the world if the sons of God did not exist yet? I suppose you might suggest that these were angels of some kind that are not part of the human family, but if so, where did they come from? God must have created them too, and certainly before the world was made, so it seems unlikely to me that that is the case.

Another thought comes from the idea that we Mormons hold that Jesus is the God of the Old Testament and references to "God" or "Lord" are often Jehovah (the premortal Jesus) acting in His father's behalf, not the Father himself. In any case, it is not relevant because the time period is still prior to the peopling of the earth and certainly before birth of any kind, yet the sons of God (and presumably the daughters too) were there.

Ecclesiastes 12:7

7 Then shall the dust return to the earth as it was: and the spirit shall return unto God who gave it.

Although this verse may not seem to clearly illustrate a premortal existence of man, there is a lot more to it, as is often the case with what God says. The Bible often talks about man 'returning to the dust,' meaning that when he dies, his body will decompose into elements that originated in the earth. But more specifically, the body returns to the earth AS IT WAS. In other words, the body came from the earth originally and so it will return. Likewise, the spirit will return from whence it came, but if it came from somewhere, it would have to be from a premortal existence of some type.

Jermiah 1: 4-5

4Then the word of the LORD came unto me, saying,

5Before I formed thee in the belly I knew thee; and before thou camest forth out of the womb I sanctified thee, and I ordained thee a prophet unto the nations.

It is hard to dispute that Jeremiah did not exist before his life in some capacity, according to these versies. The Lord specifically states that Jeremiah was sanctified and ordained BEFORE he was "formed in the belly," in other words, conceived. If man comes into existence at conception (or sometime after that), there would be no one to sanctify and ordain.

I suppose you could argue that God, knowing all things and being all powerful, would know what a being will be like and he sanctified and ordained Jeremiah, even before he existed, because he knows who Jeremiah will end up being. Of course, the counter-argument is that if God knows what and who that soul will be before he exists, isn't even that an existence of sorts?

John 9: 2-3

60

2And his disciples asked him, saying, Master, who did sin, this man, or his parents, that

he was born blind?

3Jesus answered, Neither hath this man sinned, nor his parents: but that the works of

God should be made manifest in him.

This scripture at first may not seem to have to do with anything except yet another instance of Jesus miraculously healing someone. However, it does provide a little nugget of evidence about the premortal existence. The reason is because Jesus' disciples are suggesting by asking this question that they fully accept the possibility that the man could have sinned BEFORE he was born. After all, the verse states that he was born blind, therefore if he had sinned, which caused his blindness, he must have done so prior to birth.

Now just because they considered this explanation as a possibility does not make it doctrinal, but where then did they get such an idea? I would propose it is because although the true gospel had been corrupted by the Jews, many truths still persisted, including that of a premortal existence. In addition, had their idea of accomplishment prior to birth been non-doctrinal, it would seem reasonable that Jesus would have corrected them.

1 Timothy 1: 9

8 Be not thou therefore ashamed of the testimony of our Lord, nor of me his prisoner: but

be thou partaker of the afflictions of the gospel according to the power of God;

9 Who hath saved us, and called us with an holy calling, not according to our works, but

according to his own purpose and grace, which was given us in Christ Jesus before the

world began,

10 But is now made manifest by the appearing of our Savior Jesus Christ, who hath abolished death, and hath brought life and immortality to light through the gospel:

Timothy uses a rhetorical question here to teach of Christ and how his sacrifice saves us. In doing so he talks about "our" calling, but that it was given to us "before the world began." Obviously, if we were called to something before the earth had even been created, we must have existed. Certainly, you might use the same argument I mentioned above that God knows beforehand who will be who when he does create them (at conception or birth or sometime in between) but taking all of these scriptures together (and more to come) seems to weaken such an argument.

Titus 1:1-2

1Paul, a servant of God, and an apostle of Jesus Christ, according to the faith of God's elect, and the acknowledging of the truth which is after godliness;

2In hope of eternal life, which God, that cannot lie, promised before the world began;

This is another instance of a man of God referring to the premortal existence almost in passing in attempt to deliver another message. In fact, this is really just part of Paul's introduction in the Book of Titus but provides insight about our life before birth by suggesting that God promised something at a time before any of us would have existed unless we were already there. It seems a little odd to me that God would make a promise to people that didn't even exist yet. More likely I would suggest is that we were there to accept the promise.

Jude 1:6

6And the angels which kept not their first estate, but left their own habitation, he hath reserved in everlasting chains under darkness unto the judgment of the great day.

The verses before and after this speak much about good vs. evil, but this verse points specifically to a premortal existence. It states that the angels, not people, kept not their first estate (or habitation) by deciding to leave. These are further recognized as the angels of the devil by being identified as those in everlasting chains and darkness. So when did all this happen? There is really no evidence, Biblical or otherwise that suggests it took place any time since Adam, so it thus must have been before that. In fact, the next verse explains this in more detail.

Revelation 12:7-9

7 And there was war in heaven: Michael and his angels fought against the dragon; and the dragon fought and his angels,

8And prevailed not; neither was their place found any more in heaven.

9And the great dragon was cast out, that old serpent, called the Devil, and Satan, which deceiveth the whole world: he was cast out into the earth, and his angels were cast out with him.

This is the part of the story in which Satan rejects God's plan and takes 1/3 of the host of heaven with him, although there is more insight here. Notice that they were cast out into the earth; in other words, they are here with us. But of course for there to be war in Heaven, there would have to be people/angels in heaven to fight the war. Further, there is no question that Satan has been around since the beginning. Remember the forbidden fruit? Consequently, all this must have happened before the world began in order for Satan to be here to tempt Adam and Even to eat the forbidden fruit in the first place.

Ch. 8: The Book of Mormon

The Book of Mormon is "the keystone of our religion" because the truthfulness of the Church of Jesus Christ Of Latter-day Saints rests on whether or not it is what we say it is (Benson, 1986). If it is true, then Joseph Smith must have been a true prophet to bring it forth, but it also proves that God has dealings with nations other than those in the Holy Land. In fact, if the Bible were the only record of God's dealings with men it would essentially imply that He is not interested in the salvation of those outside of Israel.

Yet, to the world of non-Mormon Christians, there can be no more than the Bible. The reasons for such a belief is rarely grounded in much more than a sort of presumptuous assumption that the Bible is all there CAN be (see Ch.2: Biblical Shortcomings). Ironically however, there are thousands of Christian denominations of all sorts, all relying on the same book (the Bible) and yet they differ from one another in their interpretation of that "one" book. In fact, the Book of Mormon even contains a prophecy that predicts its rejection by many who will say "...we need no more Bible" (2 Nephi 29). If no other "Bible" is necessary, then why all the disagreement?

The Book of Mormon speaks of the Bible and the people of Jerusalem all throughout its pages and so there is no doubt that they knew about it. These people even had a copy of what constituted the Bible at that time that was taken from an antagonist known as Laban (1 Nephi 5). However, it is also reasonable to suppose that the prophets of the Bible also knew about the peoples of the Book of Mormon. In fact, at least some of them did. There are a number of scriptures that support this idea, although they don't come out and say it explicitly, a proper interpretation of the Bible makes it clearer.

Genesis 11:4-9

4 And they said, Go to, let us build us a city and a tower, whose top may reach unto heaven; and let us make us a name, lest we be scattered abroad upon the face of the whole earth.

5 And the LORD came down to see the city and the tower, which the children of men builded.

6 And the LORD said, Behold, the people is one, and they have all one language; and this they begin to do: and now nothing will be restrained from them, which they have imagined to do.

7 Go to, let us go down, and there confound their language, that they may not understand one another's speech.

8 So the LORD scattered them abroad from thence upon the face of all the earth: and they left off to build the city.

9 Therefore is the name of it called Babel; because the LORD did there confound the language of all the earth: and from thence did the LORD scatter them abroad upon the face of all the earth.

Many are familiar with the story of the Tower of Babel in which the people of the time were building a tower with the intention of reaching heaven and were cursed to have their languages confused. Although no one really knows for sure, it seems (especially with insight from the Book of Mormon) that this was not an instant curse, but one that came on over time as the various groups were "scattered...upon the face of the whole earth." Notice that it doesn't say 'throughout the land,' or 'abroad,' but rather the WHOLE EARTH. To be fair, the "whole earth" may have been confined to the whole earth that was known to these people and perhaps not to those on other continents, but in any event people were scattered all over the place. If this were so, then there would be different groups, unable to communicate with one another, all needing to know about God and his gospel. Hence, over the course of the next thousands of years among all these peoples, God chose to inspire the compilation of a single book of scripture from different writings from a single one of these groups?

Isaiah 29:11-14

11 And the vision of all is become unto you as the words of a book that is sealed, which men deliver to one that is learned, saying, Read this, I pray thee: and he saith, I cannot; for it is sealed:

12 And the book is delivered to him that is not learned, saying, Read this, I pray thee: and he saith, I am not learned.

13 Wherefore the Lord said, Forasmuch as this people draw near me with their mouth, and with their lips do honour me, but have removed their heart far from me, and their fear toward me is taught by the precept of men:

14 Therefore, behold, I will proceed to do a marvellous work among this people, even a marvellous work and a wonder: for the wisdom of their wise men shall perish, and the understanding of their prudent men shall be hid.

This seems a rather odd scripture that we might normally chalk up to Old Testament obscurity but knowing a little about the early days of the translation of the Book of Mormon indicates that this scripture was fulfilled thousands of years after it was given. Martin Harris, Joseph's scribe at the time, took a copy of some of the Book of Mormon characters and their translation to a "learned" professor who indicated that they were ancient, true and the translation was more accurate than any he had ever seen. When Mr. Harris informed Professor Anthon that Joseph had gotten the plates from an angel, he quickly changed his mind and tore up the certificate he had just signed and told Martin to bring the plates to him and he would translate them. Brother Harris said that he could not and that some of them were sealed. The professor responded, "I cannot read a sealed book." (JSH-1) So the scripture reads differently when we realize who is who:

> *11 And the vision of all is become unto you as the words [ONLY the words] of a book [Book of Mormon plates] that is sealed, which men [Martin Harris] deliver to one that is learned [Professor Charles Anthon], saying, Read this, I pray thee: and he saith, I cannot; for it is sealed:*

> *12 And the book [Book of Mormon plates, NOT just the words] is delivered to him that is not learned [Joseph Smith], saying, Read this, I pray thee: and he saith, I am not learned [certainly Joseph was concerned about his lack of education in regards to translating ancient writings that would be a challenge even for the highly educated].*

While it may seem obvious to believers that the prophecy of Isaiah was indeed fulfilled in this story, others may be skeptical. Being skeptical is easy, you just have to believe that of all the possibilities out there, this doesn't happen to be the correct interpretation of the ancient prophecy. However, if this happens to be your view, I invite you to provide another.

> *Ezekiel 37:15-17*

> *15 The word of the LORD came again unto me, saying,*

16 Moreover, thou son of man, take thee one stick, and write upon it, For Judah, and for the children of Israel his companions: then take another stick, and write upon it, For Joseph, the stick of Ephraim, and for all the house of Israel his companions:

17 And join them one to another into one stick; and they shall become one in thine hand.

In the days of Ezekiel writings did not exist in book form as they do today. They did not have Boise Cascade to mass produce paper products or Bic® to create ink pens by the millions. Not surprisingly, the process of composition looked quite different than it does today One common way was to record events was to write on scrolls and wrap them up in sticks (Bulow-Jacobsen, 2009).

Hence there should be little mystery in the reasoning that the "stick of Judah" that Ezekiel speaks of is a record of the Jewish people which would someday be the Bible of today. However, what could the "stick of Ephraim" be? Well, according to the Book of Mormon, one thing that Lehi learned from the Brass Plates that were taken from Laban was that he was a descendant of Joseph through his son Ephraim, suggesting that this "stick" speaks of none other than the record of those people, or the Book of Mormon. (1Nephi 5:14)

Don't forget however that Ezekiel's' prophecy states that these records are to be shared. The stick that is written on for Judah is for them and "the children of Israel" and the stick of Joseph is for Joseph (his descendants) and "all the house of Israel." In our day, of which Ezekiel speaks, the Book of Mormon (stick of Joseph) and the Bible (stick of Judah) are both among the nations of all the earth, being shared

John 10: 16 And other sheep I have, which are not of this fold: them also I must bring, and they shall hear my voice; and there shall be one fold, and one shepherd.

There is no specific time-frame that has been revealed, but the Book of Mormon includes an account of the personal ministration of the Savior sometime after his resurrection. (3Nephi) This scripture is speaking of exactly this and perhaps even other "sheep" around the world that even we Mormons don't claim to know about. The typical Christian interpretation is that Jesus was speaking of those that would hear His words as the apostles spread the gospel through the known world. But a careful reading reveals that these "other sheep" will hear "my voice," in other words, they will hear Jesus Christ's voice, not His words or His teachings, but His voice.

Ch. 9: The Trinity

The trinity is a very basic concept that has gotten out of control since the death of the early apostles and the general apostasy that followed (see Chapter 1: The Great Apostasy). The faithful of days gone by all understood that God, Jesus Christ and the Holy Ghost were three separate and distinct individuals each with the title "God," all with a perfect and common purpose, to save mankind (Oaks D. H., 2017) . Yet over the centuries this idea has been skewed and while many Christian denominations view God as three in one and one in three (or some other mystical concept of multiple personalities), they ultimately argue that God is one person who manifests himself in three different ways.

Much of this belief comes from the Nicene Creed, a document developed by scholars many centuries ago in which they essentially voted on what they thought God is like (The Nicene Creed and its origins, 2016). The most ironic part about this is that these scholars were the Catholics of the day, not the huge collection of other Christian (and Protestant) faiths that also adopt this creed while rejecting the Catholic Church.

Naturally, their defense tends to be that 'we can't fully understand God, so we can't rely on common sense to determine what form God comes in.' This is further complicated by the fact that the Bible so many times states that God, Jesus and the Holy Ghost are "one." We (Mormons) understand this to mean one in purpose, not one in body, but we find ourselves doctrinally isolated in this view (Encyclopedia of Mormonism, 1992).

Ironically enough, the Book of Mormon and other modern scriptures are also replete with this phrase, but we still understand it to mean what it was intended to mean. Nonetheless, the

Bible really is pretty clear on this subject and it is difficult to understand why there is so much consensus on the side of the Nicene Creed:

Genesis 1:26

26 And God said, Let us make man in our image, after our likeness: and let them have dominion over the fish of the sea, and over the fowl of the air, and over the cattle, and over all the earth, and over every creeping thing that creepeth upon the earth.

From the beginning the Bible makes it clear what the nature of the Godhead is, although it refers just to God. However, as scholars of all faiths will admit, "God" is translated from a plural word. They will say that is referring to the "majesty" of God rather than suggesting that in fact "God" really means the Godhead. (Does *Elohim* in Gen. 1:1 mean God or gods?, n.d.). In fact, it might be easy to draw the same conclusion from this scripture alone, but others in the Bible create a better perspective.

Genesis 3:22

22 And the LORD God said, Behold, the man is become as one of us, to know good and evil: and now, lest he put forth his hand, and take also of the tree of life, and eat, and live for ever:

After partaking of the fruit of the Tree of Knowledge of Good and Evil, Adam and Eve were cast out of the garden and God proclaims that man is made like one of "us." So, who was he talking to? If God really is only a single being, why then would he refer to "us"?

Matthew 3:13-17, Mark 1:9-11, Luke 3:21-22

13 Then cometh Jesus from Galilee to Jordan unto John, to be baptized of him.

71

14 But John forbad him, saying, I have need to be baptized of thee, and comest thou to me?

15 And Jesus answering said unto him, Suffer it to be so now: for thus it becometh us to fulfil all righteousness. Then he suffered him.

16 And Jesus, when he was baptized, went up straightway out of the water: and, lo, the heavens were opened unto him, and he saw the Spirit of God descending like a dove, and lighting upon him:

17 And lo a voice from heaven, saying, This is my beloved Son, in whom I am well pleased.

This of course is the famous scripture describing the events which transpired at the baptism of Jesus Christ. If we look at it from an objective standpoint it seems rather suspicious that "God" could be one being since He is being baptized, descending like a dove and speaking from the heavens, all at the same time. He could do this because he's God; he can do anything! However, if we make it an issue of our incomprehension of God's nature, it could be explained away as simply our inability to grasp how one God could be manifest in the three separate forms at once. It gets a little harder to go down that road when you consider that the voice explains pride in His son. Why is He proud of himself and why would He call himself son? It doesn't make sense to us, not because we are incapable of understanding, but because it is sense-less. This is further understood from additional scriptures that take different angles on the Trinity.

Matthew 12:31-32

31 Wherefore I say unto you, All manner of sin and blasphemy shall be forgiven unto men: but the blasphemy against the Holy Ghost shall not be forgiven unto men.

32 And whosoever speaketh a word against the Son of man, it shall be forgiven him: but whosoever speaketh against the Holy Ghost, it shall not be forgiven him, neither in this world, neither in the world to come.

This is another puzzling scripture for those that believe that God is one person manifest in three forms. Jesus makes a distinction here between sinning against Him and the Holy Ghost. Now if He is one person manifest in three, He would essentially be saying that you can sin against one form of me and be OK, but you can't sin against the other form and be forgiven. A rough analogy might be that you will let your son use the car on Friday night as long as you are eating dinner. But if you are watching TV, then he cannot. Again, just because something is beyond our comprehension or 'doesn't make sense,' certainly does not mean that God can't do it. It seems much more reasonable however, additional scriptures considered, that God, Jesus and the Holy Ghost are in fact separate and distinct beings.

Matthew 26: 39, 42

42 He went away again the second time, and prayed, saying, O my Father, if this cup may not pass away from me, except I drink it, thy will be done.

39 And he went a little further, and fell on his face, and prayed, saying, O my Father, if it be possible, let this cup pass from me: nevertheless not as I will, but as thou wilt.

These verses, which depict the Savior's atonement are gripping and beautiful, but also very telling in terms of the nature of the Godhead. First of all, Jesus is praying to the Father, something that should seem quite odd if the Trinity is an accurate representation of the Godhead. He asks the Father, if it is possible that He might avoid the unimaginable pain and suffering that He is about to endure. If God and Jesus are the same person, wouldn't Jesus already know the answer to the question? If not, then God seems to somehow make one form of himself forget certain things. This scripture also implies that the Son has a different will than the Father. Although Jesus wishes to avert suffering for the sins of the world, He is willing to do whatever the Father asks. If the Father is himself, it seems quite peculiar that he would have a different will than himself. It just keeps getting stranger and stranger if we insist on the Trinity.

John 5:22-23

22 For the Father judgeth no man, but hath committed all judgment unto the Son:

23 That all men should honour the Son, even as they honour the Father. He that honoureth not the Son honoureth not the Father which hath sent him.

Here is another obscure idea to follow if the Father and Son are the same being. The Father apparently doesn't do the judging of mankind, but the Son does. So why then would a distinction need to be made? This is like saying God doesn't judge anyone, instead God does. The second verse makes the correct interpretation clearer that we can only honor the Father if we honor the Son, not because they are the same being, but because they are one in purpose.

John 8:42

42 Jesus said unto them, If God were your Father, ye would love me: for I proceeded forth and came from God; neither came I of myself, but he sent me.

Jesus proclaims very clearly here that He did NOT come himself, but that God sent him. This would only make any real sense if God was a different being than Jesus.

John 12:27-28

27 Now is my soul troubled; and what shall I say? Father, save me from this hour: but for this cause came I unto this hour.

28 Father, glorify thy name. Then came there a voice from heaven, saying, I have both glorified it, and will glorify it again.

This is another otherwise strangely mystical encounter between God the Father and God the Son if they were indeed one in the same. First of all, Jesus is praying to the Father, something alone that may seem odd if the Trinity was actually an accurate description of the Godhead. To add further, the Father speaks from Heaven and proclaims to the Son that He has glorified [the name of the Son] and will do so again. This idea keeps coming up but begs repeating. If God the Father, God the Son, and God the Holy Ghost are the same person, then why all the mystical interactions that seem to fly in the face of all human understanding? This alone does not prove or disprove anything for certain but taken with other scriptures it makes far more sense that we are dealing with 3 separate deities with a common purpose than some incomprehensible interaction of one being with himself.

John 12:44, 49-50

44 Jesus cried and said, He that believeth on me, believeth not on me, but on him that sent me.

49 For I have not spoken of myself; but the Father which sent me, he gave me a commandment, what I should say, and what I should speak.

50 And I know that his commandment is life everlasting: whatsoever I speak therefore, even as the Father said unto me, so I speak.

Here Jesus makes another seemingly clear distinction between himself and the father that could be described as nothing short of bizarre if one is to subscribe to the traditional Christian God. He clearly states in verse 44 that whomever believes Him is actually believing the words of the Father that sent Him to share those words. This is further driven home with verses 49-50 in which Jesus distinguishes between His own words and those of the Father. Thus the words He is sharing are not His own, but come from the Father; Jesus is just the messenger.

John 14:6, 26-28

6 Jesus saith unto him, I am the way, the truth, and the life: no man cometh unto the Father, but by me.

26 But the Comforter, which is the Holy Ghost, whom the Father will send in my name, he shall teach you all things, and bring all things to your remembrance, whatsoever I have said unto you.

27 Peace I leave with you, my peace I give unto you: not as the world giveth, give I unto you. Let not your heart be troubled, neither let it be afraid.

28 Ye have heard how I said unto you, I go away, and come again unto you. If ye loved me, ye would rejoice, because I said, I go unto the Father: for my Father is greater than I.

John 14:6 is a pretty popular scripture among Christians to claim that waiving your hands in the air and "accepting Jesus" is a one-time immutable ticket to heaven, but what they don't realize is that it clearly describes the fact that to get to the Father you have to go THROUGH the Son. For this to happen they could not possibly be the same person, could they? Well, your Christian friend might argue that to get to the Father form of the Trinity, you have to go through the Son form. That's reasonable I suppose, but verse 28 clearly states that Jesus will GO TO the Father and even says that the Father is GREATER than Him. Additionally, Jesus states in verse 27 that the comforter is sent by the Father in the name of Jesus. Again, while we cannot understand everything and failing to do so does not automatically mean it is not true, the astonishingly confusing nature of the Trinity seems to be at odds with the simple nature of the Gospel of Jesus Christ, not just common sense.

John 15:23-26

23 He that hateth me hateth my Father also.

24 If I had not done among them the works which none other man did, they had not had sin: but now have they both seen and hated both me and my Father.

25 But this cometh to pass, that the word might be fulfilled that is written in their law, They hated me without a cause.

26 But when the Comforter is come, whom I will send unto you from the Father, even the Spirit of truth, which proceedeth from the Father, he shall testify of me:

You may wonder as you read this why I included this set of verses because at first it sounds like not-so-good evidence of a three person godhead. Verse 26 however is essential and clears the muddy water.. When Jesus leaves He will SEND the Holy Ghost (comforter) who will testify of Him (Jesus) and He (the Comforter or Holy Ghost) comes from the Father. In light of other passages, we have considered, it seems most reasonable that God is not sending himself to testify of himself, who comes from himself.

John 17:20-23

20 Neither pray I for these alone, but for them also which shall believe on me through their word;

21 That they all may be one; as thou, Father, art in me, and I in thee, that they also may be one in us: that the world may believe that thou hast sent me.

77

22 And the glory which thou gavest me I have given them; that they may be one, even as we are one:

23 I in them, and thou in me, that they may be made perfect in one; and that the world may know that thou hast sent me, and hast loved them, as thou hast loved me.

This entire chapter is a long prayer given by Jesus to the Father that makes clear distinctions between them. First of all, Jesus is asking the Father for things and thanking Him (the Father) for things He (the Father) has given Him (the Son). Verses 20-23 though are perhaps the strongest Biblical evidence us Mormons have of the distinction between the three members of the Godhead. Jesus asks the Father in this prayer that those He (Jesus) prays for (specifically the Apostles and Saints) will be "one" just like Jesus and the Father are one. We know that the Saints and Apostles are separate individuals, so IF God and Jesus were indeed the same person, then what He is asking for doesn't make any practical sense at all unless we wish to put forth the case that our souls all meld together into God somehow. But if He (Jesus) is actually praying that the Saints and Apostles will be 'one in purpose' as the Father and Son, then it actually makes sense. As such, these verses make it very clear that all the times in the Bible that talk about God, Jesus and the Holy Ghost being one, does not mean they are the same person or entity, but three distinct Gods with the same purpose; ."…to bring to pass the immortality and eternal life of man." (Moses 1:39)

John 20:17

17 Jesus saith unto her, Touch me not; for I am not yet ascended to my Father: but go to my brethren, and say unto them, I ascend unto my Father, and your Father; and to my God, and your God.

Shortly after His resurrection, Jesus appears to Mary and commands her not to touch Him because He hasn't ascended to His Father. What is for certain here is that Jesus is resurrected and that He has NOT ascended to the father. If God and Jesus are in fact the same person, this seems like an unnecessarily confusing way to explain things to Mary. However, if they are not the same person, it makes perfect sense. Jesus is resurrected and then returns to His father to 'report.'

Acts 7:55-56

55 But he, being full of the Holy Ghost, looked up steadfastly into heaven, and saw the glory of God, and Jesus standing on the right hand of God,

56 And said, Behold, I see the heavens opened, and the Son of man standing on the right hand of God.

I think those of all faiths would agree that Stephen was well aware of the nature of the Godhead, being in the position that he was. Just before he was killed for the proclamation of his beliefs, he saw God and Jesus. He does not suggest some three in one and one in three doctrine, but simply states that he saw them and that Jesus was in a particular place relative to the Father. As simple as it seems, perhaps God and Jesus are in fact two distinct deities as implied by the words that are used to describe them.

Hebrews 2:11

11 For both he that sanctifieth and they who are sanctified are all of one: for which cause he is not ashamed to call them brethren,

The "sanctifier" in this verse is Jesus and those who are sanctified are us, which you can see if you read the previous verses for some better context. The point here though is that we can all agree that Jesus is not the same person as us and that we don't somehow meld into one giant being with Him, yet Paul here says that we are "one" with Him. This is what Jesus says about himself and the Father all the time, suggesting that that being "one" does not have to mean some sort of one in three and three in one Godhead.

Ch. 10: Work for the Dead

Using the Bible to present a case for baptisms for the dead can be challenging because many scriptures at best only indirectly apply, which is probably the case for two reasons.

First, baptisms for the dead would not have been performed prior to the resurrection of Christ, so naturally there is no Old Testament mention of such a thing (The Church of Jesus Christ of Latter-day Saints, 2004). In fact, the Old Testament at best only alludes to even baptism for the living. Perhaps the writers of the Old Testament were not even aware that there would be baptisms for the dead following Christ's earthly mission.

Secondly, we don't speak matter-of-factly about Temple ordinances today given their sacred nature and it should make sense that this was likely the case then as well. In fact, the Book of Mormon is even silent on the subject. However, the Bible does allude to baptisms for the dead and there is evidence that at least some early Christians practiced it (Paulsen & Mason, 2010). If the apostasy really did happen the way we Mormons say it did (see Chapter 1: The Great Apostasy), it would only make sense that it would have been practiced, having been instituted by the Apostles prior to their deaths.

John 5:24-25

24 Verily, verily, I say unto you, He that heareth my word, and believeth on him that sent me, hath everlasting life, and shall not come into condemnation; but is passed from death unto life.

25Verily, verily, I say unto you, The hour is coming, and now is, when the dead shall hear the voice of the Son of God: and they that hear shall live.

This is not a direct reference to work for the dead, but strongly implies such. It is easy to argue that the "dead" in verse 25 refers to the spiritually dead, but Jesus is in fact referring to disembodied spirits. This is easier to see by looking at the verses before (namely v. 21) and the verses after (namely vs. 28-29). In verse 21, Jesus is clearly speaking of the mortally dead and continues through with no implication that the subject has changed to the "spiritually dead." So, this being the case, the most reasonable (and in fact correct) explanation is that Jesus is speaking of the mortally dead and that they shall "hear his voice" which Obviously can only happen if He is dead, andof course He is not yet. The implication is that if they accept the Gospel of Christ (in the next life), then the command to be baptized and receive the Holy Ghost would then apply to them. Since that is not possible, the only explanation is participation in these ordinances via proxy.

1 Corinthians 15:29

29 Else what shall they do which are baptized for the dead, if the dead rise not at all? why are they then baptized for the dead?

This is a common scripture to use for "proof" of baptisms for the dead, but many members of the church think it is simply because it contains the words "baptism for the dead." This is not necessarily true because "the dead" could refer to those that are spiritually dead (as most other Christians would argue). However, Paul is discussing and testifying of the resurrection before and after these verses it and asking a rhetorical question to prove his point. He isn't really even getting at baptisms for the dead at all, he's really trying to drive home the idea of the resurrection and its significance. He is attempting to prove the resurrection by asking why the church would do baptisms for the dead if the resurrection was not real. In other words, "what's the point of the church doing baptisms for the dead if there were no resurrection."

82

1 Peter 3:18-20

18 For Christ also hath once suffered for sins, the just for the unjust, that he might bring us to God, being put to death in the flesh, but quickened by the Spirit:

19 By which also he went and preached unto the spirits in prison;

20 Which sometime were disobedient, when once the longsuffering of God waited in the days of Noah, while the ark was a preparing, wherein few, that is, eight souls were saved by water.

This scripture shows that Christ visited the spirit world after His death and "preached" to the spirits in prison. It could maybe be interpreted that he didn't actually preach to dead people, but to those in "spiritual prison"; in other words, they don't know God. This is the default argument of the standard Christian, but a further look into the wording of "By" in v.19 indicates that Jesus was "put to death…but quickened by the spirit: BY which he went and preached…"(emphasis added). In other words, He did this as a result of being dead and in spirit form. Further evidence is found in v.20 which refers to the "disobedient" at the time of Noah. Accordingly Jesus seems to have been visiting people that were disobedient in the days of Noah. That certainly could not happen unless it was in the spirit world as this was written thousands of years after the days of Noah.

1 Peter 4:5-6

5 Who shall give account to him that is ready to judge the quick and the dead.

6 For for this cause was the gospel preached also to them that are dead, that they might be judged according to men in the flesh, but live according to God in the spirit.

Verse 5 is undeniably speaking of people that are dead physically; it is difficult to interpret it another way. That being said, v.6 proclaims that the gospel is preached to the dead so that they can be judged fairly, but still live in the "other" world. That would imply that they have the ability to accept the gospel in the next life, but since they are judged as men in the flesh, their obligation is therefore the same, meaning faith, repentance, baptism, etc.

Bibliography

1914—A Significant Year in Bible Prophecy. (2018, January 3). Retrieved from Jehovah's

    Witnesses: https://www.jw.org/en/publications/books/bible-teach/1914-significant-year-

    bible-prophecy/

About the World Christian Database. (2017, November 5). Retrieved from World Christian

    Database: http://www.worldchristiandatabase.org/wcd/

Benson, E. T. (1986, November). The Book of Mormon. Salt Lake City, UT: The Church of

    Jesus Christ of Latter-day Saints.

Books of the Bible. (2017, November 5). Retrieved from United States Conference of Catholic

    Bishops: http://www.usccb.org/bible/books-of-the-bible/index.cfm

Bulow-Jacobsen, A. (2009). Writing Material in the Ancient World. In R. S. Bagnall, *The Oxford*

    Handbook of Papyrology. Oxford: Oxford University Press.

Camille, A. (2017, November 5). *Who Decided Which Books Mad it into the Bible?* Retrieved

    from US.Catholic: http://www.uscatholic.org/church/2012/03/who-decided-which-books-

    made-it-bible

Citation for Oral Tradition. (2017, November 5). Retrieved from Oxford Biblical Studies:

    http://www.oxfordbiblicalstudies.com/print/opr/t94/e1382

Comparison of Christian Religions. (2017, December 11). Retrieved from Religion Resources

    Online: http://www.religionresourcesonline.org/different-types-of-religion/compare/pre-

    existence.php

Compton, T. (2007). Apostasy. In D. H. Ludlow, *The Encyclopedia of Mormonism* (pp. 56-58). New York: Macmillan Publishing Company.

Cook, Q. L. (2008, September). Strengthen Faith as You Seek Knowledge. *The Liahona*, pp. 10-14.

Do the Great Lakes Have Tides? (2017, December 30). Retrieved from National Ocean Service: https://oceanservice.noaa.gov/facts/gltides.html

Does Elohim in Gen. 1:1 mean God or gods? (n.d.). Retrieved from Bible.org: https://bible.org/question/does-ielohimi-gen-11-mean-god-or-gods

Eberhart, D. (2009, December 14). *Quotes Concerning the Bloody Histroy of Papal Rome*. Retrieved from Amazing Discoveries: http://amazingdiscoveries.org/R-Roman_Catholic_Inquisition_Jews_Protestant

Elwell, Walter A; Comfort, Philip W;. (2001). Tyndale Bible Dictionary. Wheaton: Tyndale House Publishers.

Encyclopedia of Mormonism. (1992). New York, New York, United States: Macmillan Publishing Company.

Ferguson, E. (2017, November 5). *Persecution in the Early Church: Did You Know?* Retrieved from Christianity Today: vhttp://www.christianitytoday.com/history/issues/issue-27/persecution-in-early-church-did-you-know.html

Ghose, T. (2013, June 26). *History of Marriage: 13 Suprising Facts*. Retrieved from LiveScience: https://www.livescience.com/37777-history-of-marriage.html

Haddad, K. M. (2016). Lazarus: The Samaritan. Minneapolis: Nothern Lights Publishing House.

Keetch, V. G. (2017, March). 5 Ways to Defend the Faith (without Causing Contention). *Liahona*, pp. 44-47.

Kimball, S. W. (1983, September). Seek Learning, Even by Study and Also by Faith. *Ensign*.

Kreeft, P. (2017, December 27). *What WIll Heaven Be Like?* Retrieved from Christianity Today: https://www.christianitytoday.com/biblestudies/articles/theology/what-will-heaven-be-like.html

Matthews, R. J. (1992). Joseph Smith Translation of the Bible (JST). In *Encyclopedia of Mormonism* (pp. 763-769). New York: Macmillian Publishing Company.

McConkie, B. R. (1954). Doctrines of Salvation. In B. R. McConkie, *Doctrines* (pp. 2: 310-311). Salt Lake City: Bookcraft.

Nash, M. B. (2015, December 18). The New and Everlasting Covenant. *Ensign*, pp. 41-47.

New World Encyclopedia. (2017, December 27). *Amos (Prophet)*. Retrieved from New World Encyclopedia: http://www.newworldencyclopedia.org/entry/Amos_(prophet)

Newton, M. (2017, December 28). *Who Were Timothy And Titus?* Retrieved from Bible.org: https://bible.org/seriespage/who-were-timothy-and-titus

Oaks, D. H. (1995, May). Apostasy and Restoration. *Ensign*.

Oaks, D. H. (2017, April). *The Godhead and the Plan of Salvation*. Retrieved from LDS.org: https://www.lds.org/general-conference/2017/04/the-godhead-and-the-plan-of-salvation?lang=eng

Paulsen, D. A., & Mason, B. M. (2010). Baptism for the Dead in Early Christianity. *Journal of the Book of Mormon and Other Restoration Scripture*, 22-49.

Peter and the Papacy. (2017, October 15). Retrieved from Catholic Answers:

    https://www.catholic.com/tract/peter-and-the-papacy

Plural Marriage in The Church of Jesus Christ of Latter-day Saints. (2017, October 18).

    Retrieved from The Church of Jesus-Christ of Latter-day Saints:

    https://www.lds.org/topics/plural-marriage-in-the-church-of-jesus-christ-of-latter-day-

    saints?lang=eng

Preparing for Eternal Progression. (1997). In T. C.-d. Saints, *Teachings of Presidents of the*

    Church: Brigham Young (pp. 85-91). Salt Lake City: The Church of Jesus Christ of

    Latter-day Saints.

Randall, R. (2017, December 27). *How Many Churches Does America Have? More Than*

    Expected. Retrieved from Christianity Today:

    http://www.christianitytoday.com/news/2017/september/how-many-churches-in-america-

    us-nones-nondenominational.html

Smith, J. (2013). The Articles of Faith of the Church of Jesus Christ of Latter-day Saints. In J.

    Smith, *The Pearl of Great Price.* Salt Lake City: Intellectual Reserve, Inc.

Talbott, T. (2017, February 17). *Heaven and Hell in Christian Thought*. Retrieved from

    Standford Encyclopedia of Philosophy: https://plato.stanford.edu/entries/heaven-hell/

Tharoor, Ishaan. (2015, September 4). *7 wicked popes, and the terrible things they did*. Retrieved

    from The Washington Post:

    https://www.washingtonpost.com/news/worldviews/wp/2015/09/24/7-wicked-popes-and-

    the-terrible-things-they-did/?utm_term=.65110f24554d

The Articles of Faith. (2017, November 5). Retrieved from The Church or Jesus Christ of Latter-day Saints: https://www.lds.org/scriptures/pgp/a-of-f/1

The Church of Jesus Christ of Latter-day Saints. (2004). 1 Corinthians 15-16. In *New Testament Student Manual* (p. 385). Salt Lake City: The Church of Jesus Christ of Latter-day Saints.

The Infancy Gospel of Thomas. (2017, November 5). Retrieved from The Gnostic Society Library: http://gnosis.org/library/inftoma.htm

The Nicene Creed and its origins. (2016, July 28). Retrieved from Catholic News Herald: http://catholicnewsherald.com/faith/101-news/faith/364-the-nicene-creed-and-its-origins

Tides and Water Levels. (2017, December 30). Retrieved from National Oceanic and Atmospheric Administration: https://oceanservice.noaa.gov/education/kits/tides/tides02_cause.html

Underwood, G. (2002). The "Same" Organization That Existed in the Primitive Church. *Go Ye into All the World: Messages of the New Testament Apostles*, pp. 167-186. Retrieved from The Church of Jesus Christ of Latter-day Saints.

Vallely, P. (2010, January 6). *The Big Question: What's the history of polygamy, and how serious a problem is it in Africa?* Retrieved from Independent: http://www.independent.co.uk/news/world/africa/the-big-question-whats-the-history-of-polygamy-and-how-serious-a-problem-is-it-in-africa-1858858.html

Yee, Gale A; Page Jr., Hugh R; Coomber, Matthew J.M. (2014). *Fortress Commentary on the Bible*. Minneapolis: Fortress Press.

Printed in Great Britain
by Amazon